Essentials of
Teaching Academic
Writing

ENGLISH FOR ACADEMIC SUCCESS

Joy M. Reid
Maui Community College

SERIES EDITORS
Patricia Byrd
Joy M. Reid
Cynthia M. Schuemann

THOMSON
HEINLE

Australia • Canada • Mexico • Singapore • Spain • United Kingdom • United States

Essentials of Teaching Academic Writing
English for Academic Success
Joy M. Reid

Publisher: Patricia A. Coryell

Director of ESL Publishing: Susan Maguire

Senior Development Editor:
  Kathy Sands Boehmer

Editorial Assistant: Evangeline Bermas

Senior Project Editor: Kathryn Dinovo

Director of Manufacturing:
  Priscilla Manchester

Senior Marketing Manager: Annamarie Rice

Marketing Assistant: Andrew Whitacre

Cover graphics: LMA Communications, Natick, Massachusetts

Text credits: Tunceren/Cavusgil/Reid, *College Writing 4,* First Edition. Copyright © 2006 by Houghton Mifflin Company. Used with permission. p. 63; Walsh/Reid, *College Writing 1,* First Edition. Copyright © 2006 by Houghton Mifflin Company. Used with permission. p. 64; Nuttall/Reid, *College Writing 3,* First Edition. Copyright © 2006 by Houghton Mifflin Company. Used with permission. p. 64; Tunceren/Cavusgil/Reid, *College Writing 4,* First Edition. Copyright © 2006 by Houghton Mifflin Company. Used with permission. p. 65; Cotter/Reid, *College Writing 2,* First Edition. Copyright © 2006 by Houghton Mifflin Company. Used with permission. p. 77; Cotter/Reid, *College Writing 2,* First Edition. Copyright © 2006 by Houghton Mifflin Company. Used with permission. p. 77; Nuttall/Reid, *College Writing 3,* First Edition. Copyright © 2006 by Houghton Mifflin Company. Used with permission. p. 78; Nuttall/Reid, *College Writing 3,* First Edition. Copyright © 2006 by Houghton Mifflin Company. Used with permission. p. 79; Tunceren/Cavusgil/Reid, *College Writing 4,* First Edition. Copyright © 2006 by Houghton Mifflin Company. Used with permission. p. 81; Cotter/Reid, *College Writing 2,* First Edition. Copyright © 2006 by Houghton Mifflin Company. Used with permission. p. 104; Nuttall/Reid, *College Writing 3,* First Edition. Copyright © 2006 by Houghton Mifflin Company. Used with permission. p. 105.

Library of Congress Control Number: 2005925924

ISBN 13: 978-0-618-23013-6   ISBN 10: 0-618-23013-0

Printed in the United States of America.

23456789-EUH-09 08 07

For more information contact Thomson Heinle, 25 Thomson Place, Boston, MA 02210 USA, or visit our Internet site at elt.heinle.com

Contents

Preface

Patricia Byrd, Joy M. Reid, Cynthia M. Schuemann

The *English for Academic Success* series is a comprehensive program of student and instructor materials. For students, the series contains four levels of student language proficiency textbooks in three skill areas (oral communication, reading, and writing), with supplemental vocabulary textbooks at each level. For instructors and students, the series includes websites that support classroom teaching and learning. For instructors, four Essentials of Teaching Academic Language books, one for each skill area, provide helpful information for teachers new to teaching or new to teaching a particular area for academic preparation. The four books in the Essentials series are

- Coxhead, A. (2006). *Essentials of Teaching Academic Vocabulary.*
- Murphy, J. (2006). *Essentials of Teaching Academic Oral Communication.*
- Reid, J. (2006). *Essentials of Teaching Academic Writing.*
- Seymour, S., & Walsh, L. (2006). *Essentials of Teaching Academic Reading.*

Purposes of the EAS Series

The fundamental purpose of the EAS series is to prepare students who are not native speakers of English for academic success in U.S. college degree programs. By studying these materials, students in college English for academic purposes (EAP) courses will gain the academic language skills they need to be successful in degree programs. Additionally, students will learn about effective strategies for participating in U.S. college courses.

The series is based on considerable prior research as well as our own investigations of students' needs and interests, teachers' needs and desires, and institutional expectations and requirements. For example, our survey research revealed what problems teachers think they face in their classrooms, what teachers actually teach; who the students are, and what they know and do not know about the "culture" of U.S. colleges; and what types of "barrier exams" are required for admission at various colleges.

In addition to meeting student needs, the EAS textbooks were created for easy implementation by teachers. First, because the books were written by experienced ESL teachers, each textbook provides instructors with a range of practical support. Second, each textbook author worked with advisory groups made up of other classroom teachers, including adjuncts as well as full time instructors. In addition to reviewing the various drafts of the chapters, the advisory group members field-tested the materials with their own students to find out how the materials worked in class and to collect student feedback for revisions. This team effort led to the development of authentic, effective, and appropriate materials that are easy to understand and to teach. Additionally, each book has an author-written website that contains helpful notes about teaching each chapter, an answer key, additional quizzes and other appropriate assessment tools, and handout and overhead masters that can be printed for use in class.

The authors and editors were also aware that many instructors find themselves teaching courses in areas that are new to them or that may not be familiar to them. To help teachers in teaching the areas covered by the EAS textbooks, a series of accompanying teacher reference books presents the *essentials* of teaching academic writing, academic reading, academic oral communication, and academic vocabulary. Written by scholar-teachers, these brief, well-organized Essentials books provide teachers with highly focused help in developing their own knowledge and teaching skills.

About the Author

Joy Reid, former president of TESOL and now retired from the University of Wyoming, is currently teaching writing in the Foundations Unit at Maui Community College in Kahului, Hawaii. Joy's work on ESL writing is recognized internationally. In addition to her publications on the theory of second language writing, she is the author and editor of many ESL composition textbooks. She brings to the task of writing her *Essentials of Teaching Academic Writing* forty years of teaching experience, as well as the publication of ESL writing textbooks and resource books for teachers.

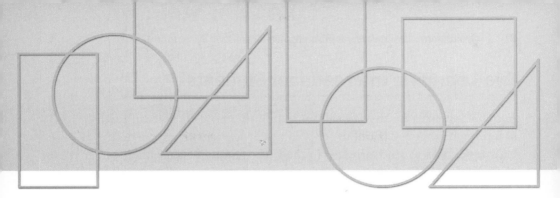

Eye Learners and Ear Learners

You have been assigned to teach an ESL writing class in an English for academic purposes (EAP) program. What do you need to know—about the course, the students, the ESL program? To answer those questions, I asked ESL teachers—experienced and less experienced, full-time and part-time—to consult with me about the contents of this guide. Our goal: to give the least you need to know about teaching ESL academic writing.

Before I begin this guide for instructors, I need to distinguish between *generalization* and *stereotype*. In this chapter, I write about two general categories of students: "ear" learners and "eye" learners. As I discuss these learners, I write about "typical" students, language problems, and solutions. Of course, I am keenly aware that although many stereotypes begin with a grain of truth, there are, statistically speaking, more differences between people in a single group than there are between two categories of people. Still, the differences exist along continuums, and although you will have some students who do not fit the following descriptions, many students from different language and cultural backgrounds do. Thus, my intention is to clarify needs and behaviors based on general tendencies, not on stereotypes.

The students discussed in this guide are those whose first language is not English but who aspire to attend college. In this guide, I divide those second language (L2) learners into two broad categories: eye learners and ear learners.

Eye Learners: International Students

Eye learners are typical international students who usually learn English as a foreign language (EFL) in school in their home countries. These eye learners choose to study English in the United States because their career goals include English proficiency. They entered the United States after a significant period of preparation, and they are supported by families who chose to send them abroad to expand their educational opportunities. Generally, these students are traditional-age (that is, eighteen to twenty years old for undergraduates), and they will return to their families and countries following their postsecondary education.

Further, international students usually understand the grammar of English and can articulate their language problems. They also may be proficient readers of English but may have fewer and less-developed listening and speaking skills. Their knowledge of U.S. culture, and specifically U.S. academic rhetorical conventions, may be quite limited. ESL teachers are usually trained to work with international students, with their cultures and their educational backgrounds, their language problems, and their language needs. Indeed, most ESL writing textbooks and teacher resource books focus on the international ESL population.

Ear Learners: Who Are They?

In contrast, **ear learners** of English typically have acquired English principally through their ears: they listened, took in oral language (from friends and siblings, TV, grocery clerks), and learned English through trial and error.

Among these learners:

1. Some have graduated from U.S. high schools
   a. with several years in U.S. schools and some English language tutoring in "pullout" programs
      OR
   b. with limited U.S. schooling and limited English language support.

2. Some have graduated from foreign secondary schools and come to the United States
   a. having studied English as a foreign language (EFL) before they arrived
      OR
   b. without knowledge of English.
3. Others have lived in the United States for some time and have attended limited part-time English classes, but they may have limited knowledge of U.S. academic skills.[1]

Further, nonlanguage differences are as diverse as with any other student group, at least in the following:

- Age, first language (L1), gender
- Education (L1 as well as the second language, L2)
- Interests, motivation
- Learning styles and learning strategies

It is probable that ear learners who do not learn well by hearing/listening may struggle intensely to learn English aurally. The language is "noise" for a much longer time than it is for learners who prefer auditory acquisition. Further, ineffective ear learners may never hear inflections; as a result, they struggle with acquiring verb tense and plural endings, and their writing demonstrates inconsistent use of inflections. Yet they often become proficient listeners of native-speaker English and make the most of their oral language skills. The result, as Mina Shaughnessy, an early researcher of "remedial college writers," posited: these students acquire a form of English—perhaps a dialect of English—that contains some (or many) non-native-like English forms.[2] This phenomenon is so common that it even has an acronym in the ESL field: BICS (Basic Interpersonal Communication Skills.)[3]

Teaching Suggestion

Teachers must consider the probable feelings of failure and fear in these students. Designing tasks and class work that can bring success to these students is the first step.

Summary

These two categories, "eye" and "ear" learners, have some things in common. Both eye learners and ear learners are learning this additional language, English, as adults or young adults. Both need guidance and structure, an organized curriculum, and well-educated teachers who can facilitate their learning. Furthermore, both international eye learners and resident ear learners are diverse in language, culture, and previous education. Both international and resident students also differ in individual aptitudes and personalities, in preferred learning styles and strategies, and in goals and motivation. The information in this guide is thus applicable for teachers and students in any L2 writing course.[4]

Further discussion of eye and ear learners continues throughout this guide. Because teachers of ear learners have fewer resources, however, this guide stresses methods and techniques particularly relevant for these students. I hope you find this guide an accessible and easy reference that you can turn to for assistance.

Endnotes

1. Harklau, L. (1999). Representing culture in the ESL writing classroom. In E. Hinkel (Ed.), *Culture in language teaching and learning* (pp. 109–130). New York: Cambridge University Press.
2. Shaughnessy, M. P. (1977). *Errors and expectations: A guide for the teacher of basic writing.* New York: Oxford University Press.
3. Cummins, J. (2003). BICS and CALP. Retrieved from http://www.iteachilearn .com/cummins/bicscalp.htm.
4. Reid, J. M. (1998). "Eye" learners and "ear" learners: Identifying the language needs of international students and U.S. resident writers. In J. Reid & P. Byrd (Eds.), *Grammar in the composition classroom* (p. 17). Boston: Heinle & Heinle.

Part **1**

Before the First Class Meeting

Chapter **1**

Analyzing a Writing Program and Preparing for Your First Class

ESL teachers beginning a new position have so much to learn—about the language program, about the students, and about the available resources. Following are some questions and answers to orient a new teacher.

What Does the EAP Program Provide?

1. Does any written material (perhaps on the program's website) about the program describe the students, the context of the program, the philosophy of the program, and other program information? Perhaps there is an operating manual—about program expectations of teachers? More specific to the classroom:
   a. What photocopying is available to you? What other equipment and materials are available (e.g., audiovisual equipment, videos, computer classrooms, student e-mail, language laboratories), and what are the processes for obtaining them?
   b. What are the program's "community standards" for teachers' office hours, teacher absences, participation on committees, attendance at meetings, and so forth?

    c. What are the schedules and processes for developing grading policies, testing, and grading; for students to evaluate teachers, textbooks, and materials; for teachers to evaluate courses, textbooks, and materials?

    d. What computer—e-mail and Internet—access is available to students and teachers?

    e. Who develops the curriculum and the skill objectives? Who chooses the textbooks? How?

    f. What processes are in place for offering curricular changes?

2. Is there a written overall curriculum for the entire program, a general, goal-centered overview of what language skills will be taught and which language skills are expected of the ESL students at the end of each class? How old is the curriculum? How often is it revised? How closely do the experienced teachers in the program follow the curriculum? Examples of goals for a typical writing course:

    a. <u>Overall goal</u>: To prepare students for the range of writing tasks assigned in degree courses in U.S. colleges.

    b. <u>Level-specific goals</u>: "Advanced beginners identify, analyze, and practice appropriate written academic sentences and the paragraph contexts in which the sentences are used."[1]

    c. Does each course in the program have <u>competencies</u> (i.e., learner outcomes)?

3. What assessment materials does the program have and use? How are new students "placed" in your class? How are continuing students "passed" to your class? What program-developed diagnostic instruments are available for use at the beginning of the class, or what materials have been used in the past to pretest the students? What instruments are available for use as a midterm examination, or what materials have been used previously for midterm assessment? What instruments are available for the final examination, or what is usually done for the final assessment of the students in your class? For example, does the program require or recommend a "group-graded timed writing examination" or "portfolio assessment"?

4. Is there a written syllabus for the ESL writing class you will teach, a day-by-day plan that directs the teacher to complete the writing skills described in the curriculum? Often the course syllabus begins with a course description that will help you with an overall perspective of the class. How old is the syllabus? How often is it revised? How closely do the experienced writing teachers in the program follow the daily syllabus?

    a. Is the syllabus required? Is there a selection of more than one syllabus? Is the syllabus mandated? Are there optional policies for parts of the syllabus? For example, is the number of required written assignments mandated? May the teacher change policies related to accepting late work?

    b. Is the syllabus tied to a specific textbook? Is there a selection of more than one textbook? Are parts of the textbook mandated? Optional?

    c. Are syllabi that were used by previous teachers of the class available to you?

5. Is there a file, a filing cabinet drawer, or a hard drive filled with supplemental teaching materials used by previous writing teachers in the class you will teach? Are there a course website, CDs, or teachers willing to share materials electronically? May faculty use but revise materials? Are faculty encouraged to share materials? Are there guidelines for teaching writing in a computer lab? Are there sample student papers that demonstrate the range of abilities at each level of the writing program?

6. Professional resources: Is a set of reference materials—textbooks, teacher resource books, professional journals—available in which you can read about approaches to teaching writing? What other options are available to you for professional development?[2]

7. Teacher resources: Is an experienced teacher-mentor assigned to you? Is a previous teacher of the class available who can talk with you, make suggestions, and answer questions? Do current writing teachers in the program have a regular schedule of meetings?

8. Equipment: Are there overhead projectors in the classrooms? Do teachers use PowerPoint, and, if so, are the materials and equipment available to you? What additional media are easy to access and use? What is the procedure for ordering or reserving AV equipment?

How Can You Be Prepared for Your First Class?

To prepare for your first class, first analyze the **assumptions** underlying the program's L2 writing curriculum. Begin by rereading the competencies, course goals, or learner outcomes for the course. Examples of possible assumptions:

In an EAP writing course . . .

1. Writers always write for an audience—a reader or readers.
2. Writing always has a purpose.
3. Written English differs from task to task, depending on its audience and purpose, but writing academic tasks includes some similar, transferable skills that can be identified, practiced, learned, and used.[3]
4. Writing and reading are deeply and integrally connected.[4]
5. Writing is not about handwriting, and it is not primarily about grammar.
6. Written English, particularly formal, academic English, is different from oral English.
7. Academic writing is almost always a test.
8. Academic writing is thus almost always "persuasive," at least in a general sense. That is, students are writing to "persuade" the instructor of their writing competence.[5]

> **Master Student Tip**
>
> Audience and purpose form the "writing context."

Second, analyze available writing **course syllabi**.

1. Study the syllabus objectives from the previous and subsequent writing classes, as well as for your own. How do they seem to fit together? What will your main focus be? Which skills will you be reviewing? Introducing?
2. Is the writing syllabus focused solely or primarily on writing? On reading and writing? On grammar and writing? Does that focus change from the lower levels of language proficiency to the higher levels?

Third, analyze **the textbook** you will be teaching with and have your own class **syllabus** prepared. Include a **policy** section. Finally, outline **weekly plans** for yourself and develop class period **lesson plans**.

Endnotes

1. Greive, D. (1990). *A handbook for adjunct-part-time faculty and teachers of adults* (Rev. Ed.). Cleveland: Info-Tec, Inc.
2. Byrd, P., & Nelson, G. (Eds.). 2003. *Sustaining professionalism.* Alexandria, VA: TESOL.
3. Grabe, W., & Kaplan, R. B. (1997). The writing course. In K. Bardovi-Harlig & B. Hartford (Eds.), *Beyond methods: Components of second-language teacher education* (pp. 172–197). New York: McGraw-Hill.
4. Silva, T., & Matsuda, P. K. (2002). Writing. In N. Schmitt (Ed.), *An introduction to applied linguistics* (pp. 251–266). Oxford, UK: Oxford University Press.
5. Reid, J. (1993). *Teaching ELS writing.* Englewood Cliffs, NJ: Prentice Hall.

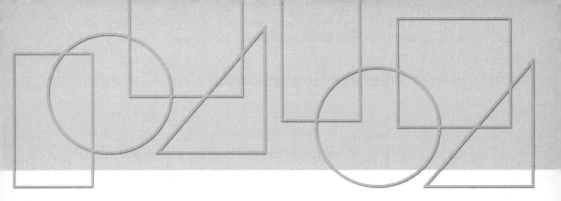

Chapter **2**

Knowing Your Student Population: An In-Depth Analysis of the EAP Writing Student

As discussed in the introduction, a majority of ESL teachers, particularly those in EAP programs, have been trained to teach international students (those students who are issued visas and come to the United States to "study abroad"). Therefore, the focus in this chapter is on those students who typically are first- or second-generation U.S. residents whose first language is not English but who aspire to attend college. These students are identified by multiple acronyms and labels including LEP (limited English proficiency); ELL (English language learners); functional bilinguals; ESL (English as a second language) in North America; Gen. 1.5 (between the first- and second-generation immigrants); immigrant students; language minority students; and L2 (second language). For purposes of this book, "**U.S. residents**" encompasses the group of students I am discussing.

Ear Learners versus Eye Learners

International students (whom I call "eye" learners) often come from prior educational systems that may have different values. One may value rote memorization, another cooperative work, still another a teacher-centered classroom in which students do not speak. In contrast, "ear" learners (a) may come from a lower socioeconomic status, (b) may face cultural attitudes that do not value higher education, (c) have probably been exposed to intolerance about their language limitations in U.S. public school situations, (d) may be less willing to take educational risks because of their previous English language experiences, and (e) may be insecure about their cultural identity. Further, they are more likely to go to school part-time and to work at least part-time outside school. They may also be a member of a cohort—a group of friends who speak their first (community) language and with whom they spend most of their time. Consequently, **the language problems "ear" learners have are different, and the solutions to those language problems are therefore different**.

Of course, the resident student group is tremendously diverse: from traditional-age college students to more mature students; from foreign high school graduates to those who have been mostly U.S. schooled; from extensive formal education in their first languages to no formal first language education. Within this diversity, however, one or more of the following general categories of resident students are present in precollege language programs:

1. U.S. resident ESL writers who are fluent and literate in their first languages but who may not have studied English: acquiring written English will be easier for these ear learners than for students who are semi-literate or illiterate in their first languages.
2. Traditional-age students who prepared for emigration to the United States by studying English, at least for a time, and who have had some education in their first language as well: these students may also find writing academic English less difficult than students who have not been so privileged.
3. Students who have not attended U.S. high schools but who have completed their secondary education in their first languages and who aspire to higher education in the United States. These students may differ in age and interests, but they have learned English substantially through their ears.

4. Students who have attended only the last year or two of U.S. high school, along with some classroom study of English prior to arrival: these students may still have learned most of their English through their ears. They may have a combination of international and resident errors that make solutions to writing problems even more complex.

5. Popularly called "Generation 1.5 students," traditional-age students who have attended U.S. public schools for a significant period of time, three years or more (and may even have been born in the United States), but whose formal ESL education has been fragmented and whose academic literacy in their L1 may also be underdeveloped.[1] Orally fluent, many consider English their primary language, and they have developed (perhaps unconsciously) language "rules," some of which must be identified, unlearned, and relearned if they are to become successful academic writers.[2]

The Strengths of Ear Learners

It is important to realize that ear learners have language and cultural strengths. Typically, these students:

1. Have relatively developed English oral fluency
2. Have highly developed listening skills, even for the more formal English of television and the public schools
3. Use phrasal verbs and idioms with ease
4. Understand reduced forms (e.g., "gonna wanna go") effortlessly
5. Speak in highly complex sentence structures naturally, without difficulty
6. Understand what's hot and what's not: the slang, the body language, the pop music, the behaviors, the humor, and the "cool" clothes of the diverse students in the schools they attend
7. Have some familiarity with the U.S. educational system, some "academic literacy," if only as more observers than participants
8. Recognize and understand classroom behaviors such as group work, conversational turn-taking, and student input during classroom discussions

9. Have had experience with
   a. The processes of registration and changing classes
   b. Writing classroom behaviors like prewriting forms, face-to-face response to the writing of peers, the overall organization of paragraphs and essays
   c. The use of computers in academic writing
   d. The use of U.S.-published textbooks

In other words, they have substantial success in communicating orally, and they know some things about the culture of U.S. schools.

NOTE: Many of these resident students share a negative attitude toward typical ESL preparatory classes.[3] When these students are assigned to ESL classes with curricula focused on the international students, their general response is strong. These classes are obstructing their educational goals; the classes are not for "Americans" as they are; and as ear learners, they do not belong in classes with "people" who cannot even "speak English."

Explanation

And they may be right. Few ESL classes are directed toward resident students. In typical ESL EAP writing classes, for example, international students are asked to write about "dating in your home country." Textbooks present grammar with terms and examples that focus on the prior knowledge of international eye learners who can discuss the issues. Often, the grammatical terminology, and even the concept of structures, is unknown (and thought to be unnecessary) to resident ear learners. Teachers speak slowly and deliberately; these near-native resident student listeners find that speech boring and even patronizing. Readings about American culture are beneath their current knowledge, and listening to the oral presentations of international students is painful.[4]

More specific to this chapter, the English language problems that resident students have with academic writing are only rarely addressed. Generally, teachers are unprepared even to read and understand the specific ear learner writing errors. In fact, the horror of the phonetic spelling in many resident students' papers is enough to contaminate the content for the teacher/evaluator. The underprepared response of these teachers is to assign grammar exercises. However, long-standing reliable research with NES developmental/remedial writers demonstrates that, at least with NESs, the results of workbook exercises about grammar structures do not transfer to students' writing.[5]

The problem seems to lie in the difference between learning the grammar of a new language and trying to remediate the grammar errors of a known language. (Chapters 3 and 4 provide longer discussions of these issues.)

Characteristics of Ear Learner English

The informal conversational English of ear learners is the foundation for many of their academic difficulties. Some of the characteristics of that speech:

- Short phrases rather than long, complicated sentences
- Short versions of questions that may use just intonation instead of question structures
- Heavy use of personal pronouns
- Use of reduced words and phrases such as "gonna" and "wanna"
- Frequent use of present tense, usually simple present tense
- Limited range of vocabulary; very limited range of academic vocabulary
- Specialized group vocabulary used to mark group membership[6]

One result of these characteristics is that many of these students have faced various levels of failure in their academic experiences. The fear of failure can eventually paralyze, and fear can interfere with, even negate, learning.[7] Another consequence is that many of the students are so successful with their oral skills that they are surprised and suspicious when they are required to take ESL classes. Still another characteristic is that these students may have delayed academic acquisition because their academic English is limited.[8] Consequently, they may be underprepared for college work. At least they are inexperienced and/or unsuccessful readers and writers. Finally, in most cases, they lack strong learning strategies and confidence, and they have little information about academic college culture.[9]

At least in part because of their language limitations, ear learners may not understand the meaning of the vocabulary and sentence structures of formal, academic written English. For example, in the following textbook excerpt, selected (randomly) from a popular undergraduate college text, academic vocabulary is <u>underlined</u>. Notice the accumulation of formal vocabulary, words that many resident students have not encountered previously. Reading researchers[10] have shown that the popular strategy of "guessing from context" is ineffective for "unsupported" reading (i.e., without intensive, teacher-based support) unless the reader understands 98 percent of the words in the text.[11] For less experienced and proficient readers who know little about the subject, academic and technical vocabulary presents a struggle. Vocabulary specialist and researcher Paul Nation has demonstrated that even with support, students have difficulty guessing from context if the percentage of known words surrounding the unfamiliar word is less than 95 percent.

In the following textbook paragraph, notice also (a) the density of numerous prepositional phrases, often in sequence (*italicized*); (b) the use of in-text citations; and (c) the passive voice (**boldfaced**). (Some words occur in more than one category.)

> The <u>evoked</u> brain <u>potential</u> is a small, <u>temporary</u> change *in voltage* on an <u>*electroencephalogram*</u> (EEG) that <u>occurs</u> *in response to specific events* (Ruggs & Coles, 1995). <u>Figure 8.4</u> shows an example. Each <u>peak</u> <u>reflects</u> the firing *of large groups of* <u>neurons</u>, *within different* <u>regions</u> *of the brain, at different times during the information-processing* <u>sequence</u>. Thus, the pattern *of the peaks* <u>provides</u> information that is more <u>precise</u> than overall <u>reaction</u> time. For example, a large <u>positive peak</u>, **called** P3000, <u>occurs</u> 300-500 <u>milliseconds</u> *after a* <u>stimulus</u> **is presented**. The exact timing *of the P300* **is affected** *by* <u>*factors*</u> that <u>affect</u> the speed *of perceptual processes*, such as the difficulty *of* <u>*detecting*</u> a <u>stimulus</u>. But the timing *of the P300* **is not affected** *by* <u>*factors*</u>—such as changes *in* <u>*stimulus-response compatibility*</u>—that just <u>alter</u> the speed with which a <u>response</u> is **selected** and **executed** (Rugg & Coles, 1995; Siddle <u>et al</u>., 1991). <u>Hence</u>, the length *of time before a P300* <u>occurs</u> may <u>reflect</u> the <u>duration</u> *of the first two stages of information processing* **shown** *in* <u>*Figure 8.2*</u>. (p. 253)[12]

Assumptions **about** EAP Writing Students

Finally, regardless of whether students are international or resident, of traditional- or nontraditional-age, from one language or cultural background or another, they have the following in common:

1. The writers have good intentions: at the very least, they
   a. want to be educated and learn how to write effectively
   b. don't make errors on purpose
   c. don't deliberately write poorly
   d. need to be socialized into academic writing
   e. are often frightened of failure
2. The writers need to be encouraged, supported, and taught.

Assumptions **of** EAP Writing Students

Most student writers believe in (at least) the following myths about academic writing:

1. The teacher knows the secret(s) of effective academic writing but won't tell them.
2. Student writing is therefore "hit and miss," and grading of student writing is subjective.
3. Every writing assignment is a brand new ball game (there are no general rules, no transferable skills).
4. Writing "formally" means copying the "fancy" language found in library books.
5. It is impossible to "see" how the important rules are used in writing models (and in their classmates' writing, even in their own writing) without assistance.

Endnotes

1. Shin, S. J. (in press). *Developing in two languages: Korean children in America.* Clevedon, UK: Multilingual Matters.
2. Harklau, L., Losey, K. M., & Siegal, M. (1999). Linguistically diverse students and college writing: What is equitable and appropriate? In L. Harklau, K. M. Losey., & M. Siegal, (Eds.), *Generation 1.5 meets college composition* (pp. 1–14). Mahwah, NJ: Erlbaum.
3. Losey, K. (1997). *Listen to the silences: Mexican American interaction in the composition classroom and community.* Norwood, NJ: Ablex.
4. Blanton, L. L. (1999). Classroom instruction and language minority students: On teaching to "smarter" readers and writers. In L. Harklau, K. M. Losey., & M. Siegal (Eds.), *Generation 1.5 meets college composition* (pp. 119–142). Mahwah, NJ: Erlbaum.
5. Muchisky, D., & Tangren, N. (1999). Immigrant student performance in an academic intensive English program. In L. Harklau, K. M. Losey., & M. Siegal (Eds.), *Generation 1.5 meets college composition* (pp. 211–234). Mahwah, NJ: Erlbaum.
6. Byrd, P. (1995). Issues in the writing of grammar textbooks. In P. Byrd (Ed.), *Material writer's guide* (pp. 45–63). Boston: Heinle & Heinle.
7. Cornell, C. (1995). Reducing failure of LEP students in the mainstream classroom and why it is important. *The Journal of Education Issues of Language Minority Students, 15(Winter).* URL: www.ncela.gwu.edu/miscpubs/jeilms /vol15/reducing.htm.
8. Shin, S. J., & Milroy, L. (1999). Bilingual language acquisition by Korean schoolchildren in New York City. *Bilingualism: Language and Cognition, 2*(2), 147–167.
9. Harklau, L. (2000). From the "good kids" to the "worst": Representations of English language learners across the curriculum. *TESOL Quarterly, 34,* 35–67.
10. Carver, R. (1994). Percentages of unknown words in text as a function of the relative difficulty of the text: Implications for instruction. *Journal of Reading Behavior, 26*(4), 413–437.
11. Nation, I. S. P. (2001). *Learning vocabulary in another language.* Cambridge, UK: Cambridge University Press.
12. Berstein, D. A., & Nash, P. W. (2005). *Essentials of psychology* (3rd ed.). (Student ed.). Boston: Houghton Mifflin.

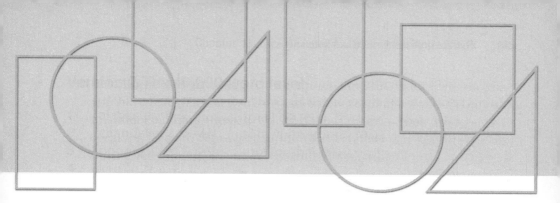

Chapter 3

Resident Student Writing Problems

Again, a caveat to begin this chapter. So little research has been done with resident students that what follows is based on (a) the published research that exists and (b) hundreds of resident student papers, classroom investigation reports (conference presentations, teacher surveys), teachers' experiences, students' comments, and other informal means of data collection. The consequence: I use many "hedges"; *"may, might, could"*; *"many, some"*; *"almost all, nearly"*; and *"probably, possible."* The reason: sufficient empirical data are not currently available, but the combination of informal data and teacher expertise strongly indicates that these errors, issues, problems, and solutions exist.

Issues about Student Error

1. Why do students make errors?
2. What part does/should error gravity play in teacher response?
3. How many errors should teachers identify?
4. What kinds of errors should teachers identify?
5. Should teachers <u>correct</u> errors as they respond?
6. How can teachers analyze patterns of student errors?[1]

First, the language limitations of resident students are evident in their writing, which almost immediately displays problems for an academic reader, even a well-trained ESL teacher. The **unevenness of register**, from formal vocabulary to conversational informality and slang, reads in some ways like a native English "developmental" writer. Examples from resident student writing:

1. Young folks usually get a better kick out of trips than older people.
2. . . . which is imparative to hang around a large number of friends.
3. . . . they will want to take off ASAP.
4. Guys like Neil Bush are destroying the American future.
5. . . . when you spend time with a couple of your close friends and there kids.
6. Don't ask me why, Because this is my personality.
7. I don't want them to worry about a thing.
8. He should of left early.

But notice that, despite the fact that these students probably have not studied the grammar of English in depth, as "eye" learners (international students) have, the previous examples demonstrate

1. complex use of sentence structures and use of verb tenses: "when you spend time" and "will want".
2. more "native-like" language than many international student sentences, which is both comprehensible and fluent for a NES.

Second, perhaps the most visible indication of resident writing is that, as their spoken language is translated into writing, residents may display **phonetic** ("ear" learned) **spelling**: "depence on," "pestimse," ["past times"] "everwhere," "look fullther," "iwan" ["I want"], "everythings," and "obstained"—errors that are so constant and so unfamiliar that they can easily turn an academic reader's heart to stone. The errors leap off the page; they demand attention. Although they are only one part of written academic work, the teacher-evaluator feels obliged to concentrate on them, with the (incorrect) idea that if the students can first learn to control the formal grammar and spelling of English, *then* they can learn to write.

Third, some **grammatical errors** made by resident students resemble grammar mistakes made by native English writers; international students would probably not make the following errors.

1. They are eager to help you, such as giving <u>there</u> opinions on things when <u>your</u> having difficulty.
2. They made copies or had the <u>employee's</u> do it.

Explanation

*Why do so many ear learners have these problems? Almost certainly, similar to other foreign-language learners, they developed language grammar "rules" (unconsciously) as they acquired English, and the results of these rules appear in their writing. These rules may, on examination, prove to be overgeneralized or false. For example, when I asked a resident student about the capitalization in her essay, she replied, "I have to capitalize the letter 'I.'" When I looked at her essay, she had capitalized every "I" including those that appeared at the beginning, the middle, or the end of a word! I simply hadn't recognized her "rule." Unfortunately, the resident students will probably not be able to articulate those rules or even agree that they *have* rules.

*Chapters 4 and 16 further discuss resident student error and evaluation/assessment.

Analysis of Student Writing

Unfortunately, academic readers may not realize that the errors of resident students are, like the errors of international students, more or less systematized and rule-governed.[2] That is, the rules may be idiosyncratic or wrong, but students tend to use them systematically. Two results:

1. The teacher cannot identify the systems (or "rules") and suggest strategies, and
2. The students believe there are no systems, so there can be no remediation.[3]

However, if students can become aware of their rules, they can compare them with the conventional structures of English. Eventually, they may be able to monitor for their errors. Below is a writing sample from a Vietnamese student, written during her first day in a first-year university composition course in response to an article about students having jobs while in college. Inflection errors are underlined; vocabulary mistakes and some idiomatic expressions are boxed. An analysis of the errors and comments by the student writer about her rules follows the paragraph. I have numbered the following sentences for ease of analysis.

(1) The main ideas of the Article is saying that because of working while going to School reduces the G.P.A. of students. (2) Some of the Reasons while students gettings jobs is because of Advertisements and personnal luxuries that the students needed during School.

(3) What the Article is saying is true about students getting lower grade in school, while working. (4) But if we try to put strict rules on College curriculas and stopping Television advertising, it wouldn't help much. (5) [Because almost all students know what they're doing to themselves]. (6) Students are awared of the lower grades they're getting but there are more to it, then just because of Work. (7) I agree, that when you get a job, your hour of studying reduces. (8) After coming home from work you felt tired and only wanted to put School words aside. (9) I have this experiences in the past myself. (10) It does reduced my G.P.A., but I'm not blaming it on T.V. advertising or anything else.

Three general areas of error bear examination here. First, there are numerous mistakes in inflection (e.g., verb endings, plurals) and verb tense or verb agreement (underlined). Some of these errors might occur because the student's first language is not as highly inflected as English, and Vietnamese does not have auxiliary verbs (*to be* (6), *to have* (9), *did/does* (10)). Consequently, the student might question whether to add a plural -*s* to "grade" (3) and might not suspect that "are" is needed before "getting" (2). In addition, even if the student had been tutored in English, it is quite possible that subject-verb agreement in English may not be a fully developed concept nor the required agreement between verbs and the agreement between demonstrative pronouns (*this/that*) and nouns.

Explanation

It is more likely, however, that many of the student writer's verb tense errors occur more from ear learning than from first-language transfer. Because the English verb tense system is complex—a single sentence, and certainly a single paragraph, may contain several verb tenses—and because this student has listened to the language rather than studied it, she may not even recognize the mistakes, even when the errors are identified for her.

In fact, while the mistakes will seem idiosyncratic to the teacher-evaluator, the mistakes may not have interfered with the student writer's ability to communicate orally. Read aloud, for instance, "*I wanna asker,*" or "*rader then,*" or this sentence: "*The students are taken their time.*" Then try reading the Vietnamese student's paragraph aloud. Listen for the reduction of word sounds or the dropping of verb endings, and, for example, think about how this student may have learned her verb rule for "taken."

Second, the student has made some **vocabulary mistakes** and has used some **idiomatic expressions** (correctly or incorrectly) that indicate her immersion in U.S. culture (boxed). During a student-teacher conference, this student indicated she had never noticed the word "why," thinking that "why" and "while" (2) were the same word ("while") with different meanings ("Like lot of English words," she said). International students would probably not make this error. Idioms used by this student, which also would probably not be used by international students who have studied English as a foreign language, include "it wouldn't help much" (4), "what they're doing to themselves" (5), and "anything else" (10) (although an international student might write "any other reason"). Also notice that two mistakes commonly made by native English writers also occur: the sentence fragment that begins with "Because" (in [brackets and **boldface**]), (5) and the use of "then" for "than" (also **boldface**) (6). Neither is a common error for international eye writers because of the different way they acquired their English.

Finally, the seemingly arbitrary capitalization needs analysis. When I asked the student why she capitalized "Article" and "School" (1), she told me she had learned that all nouns had to be capitalized. Of course, she did not know very much about nouns, but she did her best. She added that she also knew the (correct) rule about capitalizing "I," although she found that particular English capitalization rule peculiar and intimidating because capitalizing "I" made her "stand out too much" in her writing.[4]

Endnotes

1. Goldstein, L. (2001). For Kyla: What does the research say about responding to ESL writers? In T. Silva & P. K. Matsuda (Eds.), *On second language writing* (pp. 73–89). Mahwah, NJ: Erlbaum.
2. Harklau, L. (2003). L2 writing by "Generation 1.5 students": Recent research and pedagogical trends. *Journal of Second Language Writing, 12*(2), 153–156.
3. Fu, D. (1995). *My trouble is my English.* Portsmouth, NH: Boynton/Cook.
4. This chapter and the next contain information from a previously published article, "EAP resident students and error." (in press). In P. Bruthiaux & D. Atkinson (Eds.), *Applied linguistics in theory and practice.* Cambridge, UK: Cambridge University Press.

Resident Student Errors and Error Gravity

The analysis in Chapter 4 demonstrates the seemingly overwhelming language problems faced by U.S. resident student writers. So, how can writing teachers confront and treat such multiple errors in students' papers? As a beginning, they should understand the following:

1. Some grammatical and syntactic errors are more serious than others.
2. Some errors are more "treatable" than others.
3. For less "treatable" errors, students should use a native English speaker (NES) proofreader.[1]

Error Gravity

Error gravity is the name given to studies that determine which student errors are considered (a) more irritating or (b) more serious ("grievous") in their writing. Research in error gravity, based on the rankings of post-secondary academic readers, has found that, in general, error types that interfere with comprehension are more "grievous" than those that do not. For example, errors in word order, verb tense, and word choice are more likely to prevent the academic reader from making sense of the message.[2] Of these three error types, word order is rarely a problem for resident students, and incorrect word choice does not often interfere with comprehension.

Error gravity research lists the following as less serious errors: article mistakes, incorrect preposition choice, lack of pronoun agreement, comma splices, and spelling mistakes. Many of these less grievous error types are made by resident writers, often persistently and frequently. To add to the error problem, resident writer errors usually "look different" from native English writers' errors in these categories. For instance, preposition errors made by native English-speaking students—which are also persistent and frequent—differ from those made by resident (and international) students. That is one important reason why ESL students' preposition errors are more "visible" (and strange, and therefore perhaps seen as more grievous) to the NES academic reader, even though preposition errors, regardless of the error, do not usually interfere with direct communication of ideas. The table lists preposition errors made by (a) actual native English writers and (b) resident writers in a common in class writing assignment.

Preposition Errors of Native English Writers	Preposition Errors of U.S. Residents
attentive of . . .	. . . in this path
. . . guess for the answer	to invade on someone
pursuit for happiness	I use myself to another example
an affront on . . .	. . . has been used at my knowledge
no exception of . . .	. . . to stick of a headline
disagree to the argument	I arrived to the class
as a result to these problems	greatful of what they did
agree in some extent	I disagree [X]* the argument
in that bad of shape	it doesn't bother to me

*[X] = no preposition used

The first example paragraph, typical of resident student writing, demonstrates some errors considered more and less serious by error gravity research. Grievous errors: verb tense errors are <u>underlined</u>; incorrect word choices are **boldfaced** (word order errors do not exist). Less grievous errors (article use, preposition choice, and spelling mistakes) are boxed. Some errors are categorized more than once; articles and prepositions that the writer omitted are indicated in brackets: [X].

First I <u>use</u> [X] library when I **been** [X] high school in [X] past several years in america, I am still using [X] library now and I <u>realized</u> that <u>visit</u> [X] library <u>are</u> on the increase on higher education. The pupose that I visit library is such as for research, assignment, and study for myself; therefore, i think this library <u>gave</u> us good benefit **influence.** However, using [X] library is **anxiety** with the fact that many students have complin about library research skills. I can easy <u>to see</u> that happen in high school and college library: I am going to compare with high school librairies and college libraies.

Notice first that the verb errors are troublesome for the academic reader. However, read the second example paragraph aloud. Notice that when the verbs are corrected, the overall meaning of the paragraph (though it still sounds "foreign") is clear.

First I <u>used</u> [X] library when I was [X] high school in [X] past several years in america, I am still using [X] library now and I <u>realize</u> that <u>visiting</u> [X] library <u>is</u> on the increase on higher education. The pupose that I visit library is such as for research, assignment, and study for myself; therefore, i think this library <u>gives</u> us good benefit **influence**. However, using [X] library is **anxiety** with the fact that many students have complined about library research skills. I can easy <u>see</u> that happen in [X] high school and college library: I am going to compare with high school librairies and college libraies.

So while some academic readers may be irritated by the preposition and article errors, and perhaps confounded by the spelling errors, comprehension is possible—but only if the reader does not allow the errors to contaminate the content (much easier said than done).

Partial Solutions

First, teachers need to understand the level of difficulty students have learning and remediating specific English language structures, especially if their unconscious language "rules" are strongly habituated. That is, which errors are "treatable" and which are not? Which will take students a lifetime, and which can they identify, correct, and monitor with relative ease?[3] One place to begin is with article and preposition errors. Both are quite difficult for many resident writers to remediate because

1. <u>prepositions</u> do not occur, or do not occur often, and are certainly not as numerous, in their first languages;
2. <u>preposition</u> rules in English are particularly arbitrary and idiomatic;
3. <u>articles</u> do not occur in their first languages, and English article rules are very complex; and/or
4. ear learners have neither "heard" nor recognized differences between *a, an,* and *the* in English.

Clearly, if students cannot identify errors, they cannot correct them.

Teaching Suggestions

*One effective solution is to help students not only identify and correct but also prioritize their errors, based on the concept of error gravity. That is, if students understand that some errors are more grievous than others, instead of remediation being an impossible task, remediating one category of error seems more possible.[4] By dividing students' errors into these broad categories, and later perhaps into subcategories, the process of remediation seems more reasonable.

*NOTE: Later chapters additionally discuss U.S. resident/immigrant student error and teacher evaluation/assessment of student writing.

Typically, resident student writing contains phonetic spelling, incorrect or missing verb endings and verb agreement problems, and often a sprinkle of inappropriately informal idioms and language. With the help of error gravity information and their personal analyses of their writing errors, students can take the responsibility for what they believe they should remediate immediately. Some may decide, for example, to concentrate on learning about verbs in academic writing or on developing strategies for monitoring for verb agreement errors. Others may identify twenty spelling words that they misspell and that occur frequently in academic writing and devise strategies for learning them.

Next, interaction with peers, particularly native English writers, can be powerful and empowering experiences for resident writers. Peer tutors and native English friends can serve as editors and language informants for resident writers. For this strategy to be successful, teachers must first accept the fact that a native English speaker can become a valuable resource for a U.S. resident student

- without interfering with resident student learning;
- without "appropriating" resident writing;
- without being a source of "cheating" for the resident student; and
- without even "teaching" the student.

The NES can easily proofread and point out nontreatable second language errors (e.g., articles and prepositions), as well as grievous (e.g., verb) errors and *orally* suggest correct usage. This process allows the resident student the confidence and time to focus on content and organization. I advise my ESL students about appropriate approaches to such assistance:

1. Never expect a native speaker proofreader to write, revise, or rewrite your paper; the native speaker should *never* use a writing instrument.
2. Sit with the NES proofreader and learn from him or her by
   a. identifying specific problems,
   b. asking specific questions,
   c. making changes,
   d. drawing conclusions and learning.

Conclusion

No U.S. resident student deliberately turns in a paper laden with errors or tries to irritate the academic reader. Indeed, many spend much more time and energy on the language than on the content of their written assignments in their best efforts to avoid error. But for many U.S. resident writers, the task of avoiding error seems overwhelming. (In fact, the task is overwhelming.) Nor are resident students by nature lazy, unmotivated, language deficient, or cognitively incapable. Rather, these students are struggling with a second dialect (i.e., another, more formal, dialect of English), and they have very few linguistic resources and prior knowledge to aid their struggle. They need skills and strategies that will allow them to work toward effective academic writing. They need additional linguistic information, careful analysis of their writing weaknesses by professionals, and consistent support.[5]

Furthermore, teachers and students must expect that improvement in resident students' writing errors will be neither quick nor easy. Writing in a second language is an even more complex set of cognitive tasks than writing in a native language. The positive results of the time, effort, understanding, energy, and patience spent preparing U.S. resident students for the "real world" are essential and important, not only for the student but also for the college and the community, even the country. These students, five million strong, like all students, are not worthless; they are priceless. No community can afford to lose these generations of potentially productive citizens.

Endnotes

1. Ferris, D. (2002). *Treatment of error in second language writing.* Ann Arbor: University of Michigan Press.
2. Vann, R., Lorenz, F. D., & Meyer, D. E. (1991). Error gravity: Faculty response to error in the written discourse of non-native speakers of English. In L. Hamp-Lyons (Ed.), *Assessing ESL writing in academic contexts* (pp. 181–195). Norwood, NJ: Ablex.
3. Ferris, D., & Roberts, D. (2001). Error feedback in L2 writing classes: How explicit does it have to be? *Journal of Second Language Writing, 10,* 11–18.
4. Santos, T. (1988). Professors' reactions to the academic writing of non-native-speaking students. *TESOL Quarterly, 18,* 671–688.
5. Ruiz-de-Valasco, J., Fix, M., & Clewel, B. C. (2001). *Overlooked and underserved: Immigrant students in U.S. secondary schools.* Washington, DC: The Urban Institute.

Part **2**

Possibilities for the First Two Weeks of Class

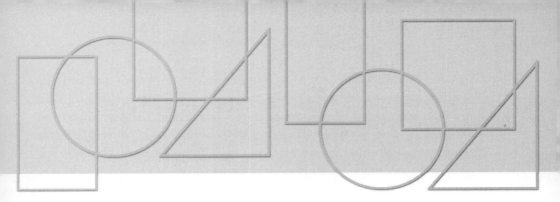

Chapter **5**

Analyzing Student Writing

The first two weeks of a course usually set the tone and rhythm of the semester, as well as the multifaceted relationships between teachers and students. Teachers establish many roles for themselves in the classroom, including, in no particular order, *coach, guide, evaluator, cheerleader, responder, expert, facilitator,* and *mediator.* In any new course, you will use the first important weeks to learn about students' writing strengths, weaknesses, and needs so that you can develop a course that fulfills both the objectives of the course and the needs of the students.

Following are suggestions for a variety of activities to use during the first week or two of classes, during which time your class membership may change. You can, of course, begin to use the textbook and the course syllabus simultaneously. But you can intersperse one or all of the activities described in the following chapters with textbook discussion and the teaching of concepts. Focus on them as community-building activities that will prepare students for the rest of the course.

Assign and Diagnose Students' Writing

During the first two weeks of class, you will almost certainly administer one or more diagnostic writing samples as part of getting to know the students' writing. In that way, you can assess individual strengths and weaknesses, formulate daily lesson plans for the first half of the course, and give students partner or small-group assignments.

Most ESL writing classes begin with a diagnostic writing sample, which (a) gives the teacher insights into the writing proficiency of the students and (b) acts as a needs assessment for the class. The diagnostic writing may be completed in class (under the pressure of time) and/or at home, depending on the teacher's needs. It may be one or two short samples during the first and/or second class meetings, or it could be a single longer piece. The samples should provide information about students' abilities to

- address a given topic for an academic reader and
- demonstrate the competencies required in the previous writing class.

1. Short diagnostic assignments
   a. Write a paragraph about your mother (or a brother/sister, friend).
   b. Select one seashell from the pile on my desk and describe it.
   c. Describe what you consider is your most serious problem in writing English. Give specific examples to support your opinion.
   d. What instruction in written academic English have you had before this class? Give examples.
   e. What frustrates you most about writing?
   f. Do you like to write in your first language? Explain why or why not.
2. Longer diagnostic assignments: Many sample topics for a single longer piece of writing can come from the TOEFL Test of Written English (TWE) list of topics (available through the website TOEFL@ets.org) or be one of the following:
   a. Write a brief report about the most serious problem you encountered during the past two years. How did you solve that problem? Use specific examples to support your ideas.
   b. Describe a favorite vacation place in the United States (or in another country). Persuade your reader to go to that place on his or her next vacation by using specific examples and details.

    c. Select a television or print advertisement. Discuss why, in your opinion, that advertisement is (or is not) successful.

    d. Assume you have a younger brother or sister who is a first-year high school student. Describe to your sibling an accurate and efficient process for evaluating written materials on the Internet.

3. As students write, you can

    a. write tonight's homework assignment on the board,

    b. walk around the class to be sure students are writing comfortably,

    c. write questions about students' diagnostic writing process on the board (see below),

    d. warn students when one to three minutes are left.

Teaching Suggestion

Following each diagnostic writing task, you might prepare students for the rest of the course by discussing their diagnostic writing processes and by asking such questions as these:

- What did you think first when you learned you were going to write?
- What did you think first when you read the topic?
- Did you begin writing immediately, or did you think, make notes, outline, and/or prewrite for a few minutes?
- Did you leave a few minutes to proofread and edit your paragraph?
- Did you have sufficient time to complete the writing task?
- How would you have improved your paragraph if you had had five more minutes?
- Did you think about your reader as you wrote your paragraph? (i.e., YOU, the teacher). They probably did not, but they should have.
- What do you think I expect from these paragraphs? (Tell them if they don't know, and list your expectations on the board.)
- Do you usually think about predicting the reader response?

Evaluate Students' Diagnostic Writing[1]

Use a holistic scoring guide to evaluate the overall effectiveness of students' writing. The TOEFL TWE Scoring Guide is clear and easy for students to understand.[2] Or you might use a three-part guide, such as the following one. Remember, the second objective of evaluating student writing is to diagnose and report to the students your perceptions of their strengths and weaknesses.

A student's writing can be categorized by using the following rubric. A rubric is a list of criteria with language that describes the range of scores for each criterion. Although you probably will not discuss the criteria you use for initial student writing, you should select criteria for each future writing assignment as you design that assignment, and you should share and discuss your selected criteria with your students. So look carefully at the criteria below; you may return to this list to form your own criteria for later writing assignments.

NOTE: Not all the words that describe a criterion may describe a student's paper, but if some of the words describe the writing, probably the writing should receive that score.

Guidelines for Assessing Diagnostic Writing		
Organization	**Content**	**Language and Structure**
Excellent: Clear introduction directed in an interesting way toward a specific reader; paragraph(s) developed with logical support and substantial data and detail; appropriate academic writing conventions: (a) general-to-specific paragraph organization, (b) successful use of coherence devices within and between sentences and paragraphs, and (c) a clear conclusion.	**Excellent:** Easy and fluid writing; fluency is no problem; diction broad and appropriate; engaging, substantial ideas that respond directly and completely to the assignment.	**Excellent:** Few noticeable errors in grammar, word order, punctuation, and/or spelling; frequent use of complex sentence structures.
Good: Obvious beginning, middle, and end; division of central ideas into smaller parts; awareness of audience; some paragraphs flawed in development and/or logic; coherence within and between sentences and paragraphs, but some choppiness occurs; conclusion often a simple restatement.	**Good:** Writing flows without much hesitation; reasonable quantity; interesting ideas relevant to the assignment with some specific detail/examples.	**Good:** Occasional errors in grammar, word order, punctuation, and/or spelling but do not affect comprehension; some use of complex sentence structure.

Organization	Content	Language and Structure
Average: Intent to develop central idea; some sense of beginning, middle, and end; occasional wandering from the topic; some development of ideas; general statements predominant; limited use of coherence devices, especially between sentences; conclusion stated simply or missing.	**Average:** Evidence of having stopped writing at times; somewhat limited vocabulary; adequate development of ideas relevant to the assignment; comprehension sometimes obscured.	**Average:** Moderate errors in grammar, word order, punctuation, and/or spelling but some errors may affect comprehension; general use of simple sentences; an occasional obscured meaning.
Fair: Limited organization beyond the sentence level; thoughts written as they come to mind; no introduction or conclusion; coherence limited to internal sentence connectors (such as *and*, *so*, or *but*).	**Fair:** Limited quantity; limited development and little specific detail; simple ideas not necessarily directly related to the assignment; simple vocabulary with frequent diction problems that often interfere with reader comprehension.	**Fair:** Frequent errors in grammar, word order, punctuation, and/or spelling that make comprehension difficult; use of short, basic sentence structures, some with errors.
Poor: Little or no apparent organization; no introduction or conclusion; little or no focus; little or no development; few or no coherence devices.	**Poor:** Little writing; very simple ideas, often not directly related to the assignment; only basic vocabulary, with frequent errors making comprehension difficult.	**Poor:** General use of phrases and/or fragmented sentence structures; frequent incorrect use of word order, punctuation and/or spelling that make comprehension difficult.

Mark and Discuss Students' Writing

Mark the papers, using the abbreviations for errors that you develop or that match a handbook or other source-text the students have. You will need to inform the students—in writing—of the terms and abbreviations you use. You might also include suggestions for correcting each error, as in the following sample:

Some Abbreviations for Marking Writing	
Sp	spelling incorrect (Correct the word and write it five times).
Agr	agreement problem: the subject and verb do not agree, or the pronoun and its reference do not agree (Correct the error immediately above the original).
F	incorrect form of the work; you have used, for example, an adjective instead of an adverb (Correct the error immediately above the original).
R-O	the sentence "runs on and on"; you need to (a) punctuate with a semicolon or a comma and a short word (*and, but, so*) between clauses or (b) divide the sentence into two or more sentences.
WF	incorrect word form (an adjective for an adverb, for example). (Identify and correct the form).

After you return the diagnostic writing to the students, spend part of the class discussing the assignment.

1. Begin by asking the students to describe the processes they used when they wrote the diagnostic, beginning with their reading (or listening to) the assignment. Ask them to be specific not only about the facts (what they did first, second, etc.) but also about how they were feeling: panicked? surprised? uneasy? List a compilation of the processes on the board, and point out agreement and disagreement with parts of the processes.

2. Then ask the students to evaluate the assignment: Were they able to complete the diagnostic in the time allotted? Did they plan their time so that they had a minute or two to reread their work and correct any errors they found (their first lesson in the important work of revising!)? Ask what they would have done differently if (a) they had had more time and (b) they could rewrite the sample today.
3. You might ask the students to revise the diagnostic or list revisions they might make.
4. Collect the diagnostics and return them (again) on the last day of class so that the students can see how much they learned!

Endnotes

1. Reid, J. (1992). *Teaching ESL writing.* Englewood Cliffs, NJ: Prentice Hall.
2. *Test of written English scoring guide* (rev., 1990). Princeton, NJ: Educational Testing Service. The "TWE Scoring Guide" is also available on the ETS website (www.ets.org).

Chapter **6**

Students Revising Their Writing

Revision is an important part of the writing process, but students almost always believe that returning to their inspired prose is an exercise in frustration, not in learning. They need to understand that

1. revision is an integral part of the learning process in a composition course and that
2. they can learn to develop effective revising skills that will improve their writing.

Explanation

Most students need to be taught <u>how</u> to revise. Revision differs from <u>rewriting</u> because when students revise, they correct only the errors in their work. They do not rewrite. Revision, of course, can include adding to or changing detail, changing the order or material in paragraphs, or eliminating parts of an essay. However, students may not be able to do more than correct "surface" language errors at the beginning of the course. Most have had very little instruction in the strategies and processes of revision. Your careful decision making about selection of errors, your marginal questions, and your summary comments on students' papers can structure student revision to build knowledge and confidence.

Student Revisions: Processes and Strategies

Because I believe so strongly that students learn at least as much when they revise their writing as they do when they write their drafts, I require and grade student revisions. I begin teaching revision the first week of class: students revise their diagnostic writing. Every major piece of writing they do must be revised.

I have developed a set of processes so that students (a) must look carefully at each mark/response I have made and (b) respond in writing to each mark. Further, the process makes revisions relatively easy and quick to grade. Following is my process:

1. Ask students to attach a cover sheet to each piece of writing, and show them how to put information on that cover sheet (name, course, instructor, title, etc.)
2. As they revise, they should
   a. use a different color ink than I used to respond to their essays,
   b. make any <u>shorter</u> revisions in response to my comments (e.g., spelling and punctuation errors) directly above the error, and
   c. make <u>longer</u> revisions ("write two or three sentences of specific detail to support this point") on the *back of the previous page.*

Back of previous page	
longer revisions needed (put on the back of the previous page)	*small errors* (put the correction immediately above the error)

3. Revision includes responding to every mark or comment I have made. For example,
   a. I mark an error. Correct it either just above the error, or if the correction is longer, on the *back of the previous page.*
   b. If you don't understand the error or don't know how to correct it, write me about the error on the *back of the previous page,* opposite the error.
   c. I mark and correct an error. Write OK next to the correction if you agree with the correction.
   d. If you don't agree with the correction, write me why on the *back of the previous* page opposite the correction.

e. I ask a question. Answer specifically on the *back of the previous page*, opposite the question.

f. I make a suggestion. If you agree, fulfill the suggestion on the *back of the previous page*, opposite the suggestion.

g. If you disagree with my suggestion, write me why on the *back of the previous page*, opposite the suggestion.

If students learn to revise in this way, you will be able to see immediately, without turning pages back and forth, without searching from front to back of the writing, whether the student has revised and how successful the revisions are.

NOTE: The first time you "grade" revisions, you might want to take extra time to see what the students are actually doing: whether they understand your marks, respond to them appropriately, and understand the processes of completing the revisions correctly.

Once students understand the process, you should be able to simply spot-check to see whether they have revised appropriately, and grade the revision accordingly. I tend to check some students' revisions more carefully than others': papers with lower grades, papers written by students who often do not revise well, and students who are having other problems in class (e.g., attendance, participation).

Here are two sample student revisions:

Sample I

Teacher Responses in the Margin	Student Draft
Title is not the main idea	**Important Sources of Knowledge**
"Travel" is a non-count word: "The purpose of travel," but not "a travel"	Many people like to travel during their vacations. They spend their vacations at a beach, a mountain, or other places where they usually do no go. Main purpose of a travel is to have a fan during vacations. But a travel also gives us some knowledge. The one of reasons why a travel can
increase?	gain our knowledge is that we can see real things such as buildings, festivals, and people, and we might or might not get different images from
repeats	books or pictures in order to see real things. We also can gain our knowledge from our hearing,

*For example,
**that it (what?)
memorize? memories?
remember?

smelling or tasting through a travel. *___ The other reason is **easy for us to memolize. We have many experience through a travel, and those experience can be memolized as our knowledge easier than reading books. Travel is not only a fun but also a good study to gain valuable knowledge.

Longer Student Revisions
[back of previous page]

Short Student Revisions

Travel for Vacation!

Many people like to travel during their vacations. They spend their vacations at a beach, a mountain, or other places where they usually do **not** go. **The m**ain purpose of a travel is to have **X** fun during vacations. But **X** travel also gives us some knowledge. **X One** of **the** reasons why **X** travel can **increase** our knowledge is that we can see real things such as buildings, festivals, and people, and we might **X X X** get different images from books or pictures **X X X X X X**. We also can gain **X** knowledge from **X** hearing, smelling or tasting through **X** travel. **(1 + 2) The other reason is Easy for us to memolize.** We have many **experiences** through **X** travel, and those **experiences** can be **remembered** as our knowledge easier than reading books. Travel is not only **X** fun but also **X** good study to gain valuable knowledge.

1. For example, we might hear the song of a new bird, or smell the blossoms of an unknown tree, or taste foreign foods.

2. The other reason is that we easily remember things from travel.

Sample II

Teacher Responses in the Margin	Student Draft
	Should Cheaters Be Dismissed from College?

Should Cheaters Be Dismissed from College?

Cheating people should not be dismissed from college.** Negative reward for wrong doing is needed but dismissed is too much.* But cheating students for the exam should be punished. They should fail in that class only. Retaking the class is a wasted time and money. Punishment slows down the *** reaching goal of life. For example, my brother, a fourth year medical student was caught cheating in Chemistry final exam. He let his roommate look at his answers before he handed in the test to the instructor. Both of them failed that class. They felt ashamed of it and promised not to do it again.

Teacher Responses in the Margin:

* because ...?
on an

not related to topic
**Use as sentence #2
*** the student's reaching his goal.
on his

cut: not necessary

Longer Student Revisions
[back of previous page]

1. because that punishment is too great for cheating.
2. student's reaching his goal, and it might even ruin his life.

Short Student Revisions

Should Cheaters Be Dismissed from College?

Cheating people should not be dismissed from college. Negative reward for wrong doing is needed but **dismissal** is too much (1). It will slow down the (2) But cheating students on an exam should be punished. They should fail in that class only. For **example, my** brother, a fourth year medical **student,** was caught cheating **on his** Chemistry final exam. He let his roommate look at his answers before he handed in the test to the instructor. Both of them failed that class. They felt ashamed and promised not to do it again.

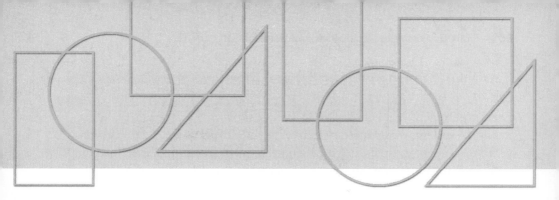

Chapter 7

Lesson Plans

Here's the question that can result in successful lesson planning: What learning opportunities can I offer students in class that they can't get (or get as easily or effectively) outside the classroom? In contrast, I ask myself, What can students learn just as efficiently outside of class? worksheets? silent reading? individual work? irrelevant conversation?

So: What can the classroom offer students? From the teacher:

- Accurate and appropriate feedback
- Cross-cultural information (including academic culture)
- Explicit answers to students' questions
- Explanations of directions and assignments
- Focusing and prioritizing information
- Real-world information and its relationship to authentic academic writing
- Support and scaffolding
- Skills and strategies training

And from peers:

- Feedback from an authentic reader
- Support of a community of writers
- A gathering of minds for discussion and learning

This chapter outlines a process for considering and designing lesson plans with objectives linked to your teaching philosophy.

The Importance of Lesson Plans

Even experienced teachers design daily lesson plans. They consider the needs of students and course objectives as their foundation. A lesson plan is more than a list of topics; it is a coherent, sequenced series of activities that will result in students' achieving the teacher's class objectives. A lesson plan:

- Formulates daily objectives that build toward the course goals (see the previous paragraph)
- Selects and sequences materials and activities that relate class activities to those goals
- Prioritizes and organizes the materials so that they are transparent for the students
- Decides on interactional patterns that lend variety to the class

   For less experienced teachers, a lesson plan also:

- Assists the teacher in preparing for class
- Demonstrates the complexity of teaching
- Focuses on the relationship between overall objectives and class materials/activities
- Provides a record for assessment by the teacher after the class

   Because you already have analyzed the textbook and written a rough draft of the semester's syllabus, you know the program goals and the objectives for your course and have some idea of the process to achieve those objectives. You can now plan your classes, day to day, toward the goals for the course and use the textbook to both frame and support your plans.

Design a Lesson Plan for the First Day of Class

Planning is essential for successful teaching. Lesson plans should be written, and they may be formal or informal. The amount of detail depends on the individual teacher, but enough should be written to result in a class that is clear, coherent, and useful. Underlying any fifty- or ninety-minute lesson plan are the following:

1. Knowledge of what you will teach (what will the class learn today?)
2. One or two major objectives (not more!) for the class
3. Dividing the class period into three or four different sections of approximately ten to twenty minutes each
   - To keep students' attention (variety being spicy)
   - To teach toward different student learning styles (e.g., auditory, visual, kinesthetic, group)
4. Varying activities, as well as student and teacher participation:
   - teacher lecture
   - teacher-class discussion
   - teacher uses media materials
   - student work (individual, partners, small group)
   - student-led class work (individual, partners, small group)
   - students use technical/media materials
5. Materials needed for the class (handouts? PowerPoint?)
6. Appropriate time for the assignment (and explanation) for the next class
7. Flexibility built in (the "just in case" factor) for the teacher's discovery that:
   - Students need more (or less) work on an objective
   - Some students are unprepared for one or more sections of the class
   - Students bring up immediately a learning task that is essential
8. Space for comments, teacher assessment after the class (for future reflection and use)

Following is an example of a suggested lesson plan format (with condensed spacing to save space on the page).

Week #_____ Date _____ Objective(s) _____

Time _____ min. Activity Type _____

Materials Needed _____

Explanation _____

_____

_____

_____

Time _____ min. Activity Type _____

Materials Needed _____

Explanation _____

_____

_____

_____

Time _____ min. Activity Type _____

Materials Needed _____

Explanation _____

_____

_____

_____

Comments _____

_____

_____

_____

A completed lesson plan for the first day of class (fifty minutes) follows. Notice that the form differs slightly from the previous form but that the categories remain the same.

Lesson Plan: First Day of Class

Week # 1   Date _____   <u>Objective</u>(s): Introduction, Policy Sheet, Diagnostic and discussion

High Intermediate Writing Class

*<u>Before Class:</u>

Prepare handouts.
Write a brief outline of today's class on the board.
On the opposite side of the board, write the assignment for
   the next class.
Buy textbook, materials.
Read assignment in textbook

*<u>Class:</u>

5 minutes: Introduction

   Introduce course, self. Point out information on the board and
   explain that it will be there each day.
   Welcome class.
   Take roll and verify pronunciation of names (mark absentees; take
   students' names not on the roll).

10 minutes: Policy Sheet (handout)

   Read aloud and go over with students.
   Answer students' questions.

20 minutes: Diagnostic

   Introduce and explain diagnostic process.
   Handout: diagnostic.
   Answer students' questions.
   As students write, try to learn some of their names.
   Collect diagnostic.

10 minutes: Discussion of Diagnostic [as long as time permits]

> Ask students:
>> What was easy? Difficult? What problems did you have? Did you finish?
>> Did you think about ME before you wrote? (Why or why not?)
>> What do you think my expectations will be?

5 minutes: Assignment for Next Class

> Go over with students (read from the board).
> Answer students' questions.

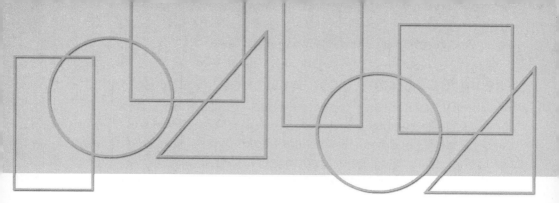

8

Setting the Themes of the Course

Use the first weeks to explain your teaching and classroom priorities. Students should understand that (a) learning takes place best when learners recognize the "real world" reasons for learning (e.g., to communicate well in the workplace) and (b) new learning is built upon former learning. Approaches to achieve these include the following.

Classroom Community

You and the students form a classroom community in which

- each student contributes talents and strengths and
- collaboration and cooperation are integral.

Discuss with your students the belief that (a) learning does not take place where fear is present, (b) learning occurs most easily in a classroom atmosphere free of fear (though perhaps not of occasional anxiety!), and (c) a close classroom community supports its members.

The Buddy System

As a corollary to classroom community, once your class roster is fairly stable, assign each student a partner in the class. Make the choices arbitrary, but try to avoid "buddying up" obvious friends. If possible, assign buddies of the same gender (to eliminate potential problems). Explain that students should check with their "buddies" before they contact the teacher with questions about the class, assignments, and so on. Thus, students become responsible for at least one other student in the class; this is the start of the "community of writers." It is also the first step in achieving classroom community (which does not occur easily among strangers).

- Buddies exchange contact information and are responsible for contacting one another to ask questions about assignments, to find out about what happened in class in the event of an absence, and to support each other during the course.
- In the first major assignment, this buddy is the reader; later, do group work with two sets of buddies, thus expanding the sense of community in the class.

The Student-Teacher Contract

Students may be interested in hearing that teachers as well as students have responsibilities throughout the course. Some teachers work this information into a contract that both they and their students sign. Here are the responsibilities I discuss with my students:

1. Students are responsible for their own learning; they should commit to
   a. making this class relevant to their needs and interests;
   b. learning about themselves and their writing strengths through written reflection;
   c. developing individual strategies for effective writing processes;
   d. learning, risking, and practicing the types of writing they will encounter in their future academic classes;
   e. building skills, and then demonstrating, applying, and transferring those skills;
   f. asking the teacher or other students for more information when they do not understand an assignment or a concept.

2. The teacher is responsible for
   a. communicating clear course objectives;
   b. developing a well-planned curriculum and daily classes;
   c. assuming multiple roles: teacher, facilitator, mentor, responder, coach, evaluator;
   d. providing authentic, relevant academic writing assignments;
   e. making available clear criteria for writing tasks and evaluation;
   f. providing professional intervention and assessment;
   g. giving feedback on student writing promptly and returning student work promptly so that students can learn from one writing assignment before proceeding to the next.

The "Social-Cognitive Approach" to Writing[1]

Of the several approaches to teaching EAP writing, the social-cognitive approach focuses on how to write for different academic purposes and for different academic readers-audiences. In other words, it

1. focuses on the practical and the political atmosphere of the writing context;
2. allows students access to the expected academic writing conventions of academic writing;
3. considers the fact that many inexperienced writers, particularly those from minority groups, are simply unaware of appropriate U.S. academic writing conventions;
4. operates on the assumption that students must therefore be explicitly taught those specific tasks rather than simply be "expected" to know them. For instance,
   a. How do you fill out a form if you have never seen it and don't know what is expected?
   b. How do you write a parody or a sonnet (or a technical report, or an anthropology research paper) if you have never "noticed" what the writing conventions and reader expectations are for each?
   c. How do you write a laboratory report or research paper if you have never been taught or even "noticed" the academic writing "conventions"?

5. forms the foundation of the course around the concepts of **audience** and **purpose**—the "mantras" you will probably talk about with students every day of the course;

   NOTE: While the "real" reader in this class is no mystery to the students (the instructor), you may need to tell them that their suspicions are correct.

6. teaches that academic writing is almost always a test of students' abilities to demonstrate their knowledge of a topic, so students need to learn that one major purpose of their writing is to discover the expectations of their reader (the evaluator/instructor) and how they might fulfill those expectations;

7. explains that the reader for their writing in this course (the instructor) is also the designer of the assignment, so in this course, students should understand that
   a. their competence in both their English language and the content of their writing must be demonstrated, and
   b. the expectations of the instructor/evaluator include a demonstration of their academic writing competence

Explanation: The Social-Cognitive Approach

Teaching writing skills in the social-cognitive approach is, in some ways, like a Montessori approach (in which, for instance, there are twenty-six small, identified—and noticed—steps to use in order to wash your hands successfully). For ESL writing, it is the teacher's responsibility to make writing tasks, formats, and writing conventions visible to the students, to teach students to notice specific writing skills rather than to simply assign writing.

Students are taught that writing for different purposes and different "discourse communities" (readers-audiences) requires differences in overall and inner paragraph organization, word selection, use of evidence, types of evidence, and so on. In other words, the writing that students will do during this course will not be just the famous "five-paragraph essay." For example, a letter to the editor ("public writing" to express personal opinion) has different rhetorical and linguistic conventions than does a psychology research paper (academic writing for a grade) or proposal or memo.

But students also learn and practice both <u>transferable</u> and <u>specialized</u> skills. That is, whereas some academic writing conventions change with the writing assignment, some conventions can be used in many kinds of academic assignments. These conventions are both organizational (rhetorical) and language-based, according to the writing situation. They can include the following:

note taking from spoken and written texts	short answers to questions	using the Internet
analysis of texts	persuasive techniques	using the library
using interviews	using surveys	analyzing language use
using references	analyzing conventions	taking in-class writing exams

And students learn to analyze such questions as these:

- How does purpose interact with genre (writing type and its conventions) and reader(s)?
- How is the writer's intention constrained by the reader(s) and the topic?
- What differences in writing processes exist in producing different genres?

Persuasive Writing

Another insight for students is that all academic writing is more or less persuasive—in a general sense of the word. In one course, for example, students write to persuade an instructor that they understand the course material, to persuade a teacher/evaluator that their writing skills merit a high grade, and to persuade fellow students to change their opinions about an issue.

General versus Specific

Another ongoing theme of any writing class is the continued spiraling of the concepts of general and specific in student writing. For whatever reasons, inexperienced writers have trouble developing paragraphs with specific detail. Yet it is essential to teach students about the following:

- Narrowing and focusing topics (from general to specific)—choosing a "piece of the pie"—and thus avoiding the ironic problem of not having enough words because the topics are too "big" (general)
- Using evidence (specific facts, examples, and other evidence instead of repeating generalities) that will persuade the reader(s) of the credibility of the ideas
- "Showing" instead of merely "telling" the reader(s) by using memorable (specific) <u>detail</u> to interest the readers

Particularly in paragraph organization and in the use of evidence in paragraphs, students must understand that merely asserting an idea does not validate a statement in academic writing. Instead, the idea must be supported (as the legs of a table support the table) by facts, examples, description, and experience—plus specific details to illustrate the facts and examples, the descriptions and experiences. This concept is truly foreign, even to many native English speakers (NESs).

Following are examples of using the concepts of general and specific as you teach paragraph and essay organization. The exercises vary by level of language proficiency.

1. Play the "universe" game: "I live in the universe, galaxy, solar system, Earth, North America, . . ." to demonstrate going from general to specific.
2. Outline everything you do on the chalkboard, on handouts, on overhead transparencies, and in PowerPoint presentations so that students can see, every day, the way general and specific "work."
3. Give students three to five subjects; call it the "whole pie" (or "cake"). Ask them to divide each subject into eight "pieces" (topics). Start by doing one on the chalkboard, and show students in an outline form the way each topic is less general than the subject but just as general as the other topics. Then ask students to work with a partner.

Subjects	"More specific" ("kinds of") categories
Pets:	dogs, cats, birds, snakes, etc.
Pizza toppings:	double cheese, mushroom, anchovy, green pepper, etc.
Computer products:	monitor, laptop, hard drive, server, PC, desktop, etc.

4. Show students how a subject can be "narrowed" and then become "most general" for more specific categories.

Subjects	"More specific" ("kinds of") categories
Dog breeds:	dashund, sheltie, golden retriever, Labrador retriever, collie, schnauzer, etc.
Computer product brands:	Dell, Microsoft, Gateway, Verbatim, TDK, AOC, etc.
Computer laptop brands	Hewlett packard, Lexmark, NEC, Viewsonic, etc.

5. Demonstrate the general-to-specific concept with subjects that are a little more difficult and show how each might be divided into many pie/cake "slices:"

Subjects	"More specific" ("kinds of") categories
Major fields: |	physics, biology, mathematics, geography, engineering
Engineers: |	mechanical, electrical, computer, industrial, construction, etc.
Physics:	nuclear, quantum, statistical, astro, etc.
Media (pl.): |	television, radio, newspapers, magazines, films, etc.
Television programs:	reality, drama, situation comedy, talk, news
OR Television brands:	Sony, Panasonic, JVC, MGA
OR Television screen sizes:	10", 14", 24", 60"
OR Television situation comedies:	*Friends, Everybody Loves Raymond, Will and Grace, Frasier*, etc.
OR Television reality programs:	*Survivor, Fear Factor, The Apprentice*
OR Television talk shows:	*Oprah, Ellen DeGeneres, Dr. Phil, Montel Williams*

The Modified Portfolio Approach

Students usually work with their writing again and again, drafting and revising, and revising even their "final" drafts. A "modified portfolio" approach is one way to (a) reward those students who have committed to the draft-and-revise process to develop their writing skills and (b) show students how much they have learned by having them return to earlier writing. That is, once or twice during the semester, the teacher and/or the students choose one or two previously written assignments to revise and rewrite for an <u>additional</u> grade.

To prepare students for this approach, require them to keep everything in a folder: their drafts, their gathered information, the related exercises, "final" drafts, and their graded revisions. At midterm and during the last two weeks of class, students can spend time selecting, analyzing, perhaps expanding, revising (again), and rewriting an assignment they are familiar with. The advantages:

- Students return to writing they have already revised and discover for themselves that there is more work to be done.
- Students learn that they have learned more since they wrote the original assignment and can apply their new learning to that writing task.
- Portfolio assignment grades are almost always higher than the original grades, demonstrating to students that they have learned skills they can put to work on these and future writing tasks.
- When students improve their writing, the sense of satisfaction is great, and their self-confidence increases as well.
- At the busiest times of the semester, students can feel comfortable with the work they are doing in their writing class.

NOTE: The portfolio assignment can also function as a midterm or a final examination.

Following is a sample assignment for a portfolio paper.
Background: Advanced Writing, near the end of the sixteen-week semester
Assignment: Portfolio Essays as Final Exam

Portfolio Essay Assignment

A portfolio is a folder that contains the best work of the photographer, the model, the artist, or the writer. Your portfolio will demonstrate the best academic writing you can do. It will also serve as your final examination in this class.

Assignment: Carefully reread the essays and reports you have written this semester. Choose ONE essay or report that you will expand and revise for half of your portfolio grade. I will choose another of your essays/reports for you to expand and revise for the other half of your portfolio grade.

Directions: For each essay or report, you will add one page of text.

NOTE: You may narrow your thesis statement for your original essay/report, or you may keep the same thesis statement, but you may not expand it. That is, the additional page of text can occur in one or more of the following:

- Additional examples or information or detail in existing (background or body) paragraphs
- Not less than one or two additional paragraphs
- More sources, direct quotations, and paraphrases
- Non-text materials

Criteria for Evaluation of Your Portfolio Essays

1. Demonstration of the ability to follow directions and fulfill the assignment
2. Appropriate overall and inner-paragraph organization
3. Use of adequate evidence and detail
4. Accurate use of sources and citations
5. Minimal language and sentence structure problems
6. Development of coherence skills through the use of transitions and paragraph hooks

Endnotes

1. Johns, A. M. (1999). Opening our doors: Applying socioliterate approaches (SA) to language minority classrooms. In L. Harklau, K. M. Losey., & M. Siegal (Eds.), *Generation 1.5 meets college composition* (pp. 159–171). Mahwah, NJ: Erlbaum.

Part **3**

Classroom Methods and Activities

Chapter 9

Applications of General and Specific: Teaching Essay Maps and Summaries

Using General and Specific in an Essay Map

You can teach students of all language proficiencies to apply the concepts general and specific to academic writing by showing them how outlining separates the general from the specific (and the more specific). The typical outline form for organizing materials (below) is called an essay map. An example follows.

<u>Background</u>: Advanced Writing Course, first writing assignment of the semester

<u>Writing Assignment</u>: Expository essay informing readers about one of the Bill of Rights of the U.S. Constitution

Essay Map[1]

(General vs. Specific Outline)

Thesis Statement (the last sentence in the introduction): This essay focuses specifically on freedom of religion and freedom of the press, two of the most valued liberties in the United States.

> Topic Sentence(s), Background Paragraph: Many political leaders, including Thomas Jefferson, were concerned that the proposed U.S. Constitution did not specify protection or privileges for citizens. Thus the Bill of Rights was written.

> Topic Sentence, Body Paragraph #1: The First Amendment of the Bill of Rights clearly guarantees people the right to practice any religion or none at all, but expressions of different religions can create problems in our society.

> Topic Sentence, Body Paragraph #2: Freedom of the press constitutes another important aspect of the First Amendment.

Concluding Sentence: (the last sentence in the conclusion paragraph): Without the insight of the framers of the Constitution, the United States would not have so many opportunities to value freedom and democracy.

Following are several exercises that can help students discover the differences between general and specific. Each exercise is preceded by contextual information about the level of the course in which the differences were successfully taught.

Example Exercise 1

Background: Low Intermediate, thirteen weeks into a sixteen-week semester

Assignment: Write a paragraph about managing your time.

Write Your Major Points and Supporting Details[2]

Use the notes from your discussion to choose three major points that explain or prove your topic sentence. Write the major points and the supporting details in this chart:

Topic Sentence	
First Major Point:	Supporting Detail:
	Supporting Detail:
	Supporting Detail:
Second Major Point:	Supporting Detail:
	Supporting Detail:
	Supporting Detail:
Third Major Point:	Supporting Detail:
	Supporting Detail:
	Supporting Detail:

Example Exercise 2

Background: High Intermediate Writing, a month into a sixteen-week semester

Assignment: Write an evaluation expository essay

After completing an essay map, the student listed some "WH" questions that would help him develop his controlling ideas. Next to each question, he listed the supporting details that answered the question (see the completed table that follows).

Product: Running Shoes[3]

Brands/Websites: Nike (A) and Saucony (B)
Thesis Statement: Nike, brand A, better markets its product to consumers through increased visual appeal, readability, website layout, and product information.

Topic Sentence #1 (Background Paragraph): These four criteria are essential in evaluating commercial websites.

Questions	
What is visual appeal?	Definition: something attractive to the eye
Why is it important?	Explain: images are the first thing we notice in a webpage.
What is readability?	Define: easy to read. Explain western reading patterns: left to right, top to bottom).
Why is it important?	Explain: Makes it easier to access information (example of website reader program for the blind.
What is layout?	Define: how images are organized on the webpage.
Why is it important?	Quote Explanation from source #2.
How much product information should a website provide?	Paraphrase information from source #1. Share personal experience.
How do you know consumers care about these criteria?	Discuss survey. Give number of people surveyed, ages, general responses.

Teaching Summary Writing

Another use of general versus specific occurs when students summarize; they need to be able to distinguish main ideas from supporting details in their reading. Summarizing is an essential college skill, but it also seems deceptively easy. In fact, academic summary writing is culturally based, so student writers must understand not only the content of the material to be summarized but also how to fulfill the expectations of the reader(s). For that reason, writing effective summaries is a skill that students should start to practice at the lower levels of language proficiency. To accomplish this, teachers should lead students through increasingly sophisticated summary skills from proficiency level to proficiency level.

Summary Writing for Low Language Proficiency Students

Students with limited language proficiency can write the main ideas of a reading passage. Following is one process that usually results in successful summaries:

1. Read the material twice, first quickly for the main ideas, and then a second time to underline and/or take notes about those main ideas.
2. Identify the thesis and topic sentences (or headings and subheadings). They will form the foundation of the "main ideas" (the "general ideas") of the summary.
3. Put the main ideas into clear, concise sentences, using some vocabulary from the original material.

Here is another exercise that students with lower language proficiency can use effectively as they write a summary:

1. They read a short passage written on the first two-thirds of a vertical page.
2. They cover the passage and write keywords and phrases they remember on the remaining third of the page.
3. They return to the reading to see whether they missed any of the main ideas and share and discuss their selected main ideas
   a. with a partner, with a small group, or
   b. with their instructor in a whole-class discussion.

Finally, students can learn the basic rules and write a single-sentence summary:

1. Write the title and the author's name early in the first (in this case the only) summary sentence.
2. Use appropriate punctuation and capitalization in that sentence.
3. Write only the main ideas in the original material: do not write your opinions or ideas.

Summary Writing for Intermediate Language Proficiency Students

At the high intermediate level, students can write successful summaries for a variety of written materials, and they can learn the differences between paraphrasing and quoting directly. These students can use the following guidelines:

1. Carefully read the original source. Use a dictionary or ask your instructor to clarify terms or concepts you cannot understand in context.
2. Identify the main ideas and essential supporting details.
3. On another sheet of paper, take notes about the important ideas. Do not copy complete sentences.
4. Make sure each summary has a beginning, a middle, and an end. In that way, the summary reflects the beginning, middle, and end of the original material.
5. In the summary, paraphrase some of the words used in the original material.
6. Use keywords from the original material in the summary.
7. Combine more than one of the main ideas from the original material into a single sentence to reduce overall word count and repetition in a summary.
8. Use only your notes to begin to write your summary.
9. At the beginning of your summary, state the source and the main idea of the entire passage, and use correct punctuation and capitalization.
10. Include all main idea(s) in your summary (usually in the order they were originally presented).
11. Include only the supporting details that are necessary to understand the main points.
12. Omit personal opinions.

13. Use cohesion devices to help your summary read smoothly.
14. Check to be sure that the summary is
    a. objective,
    b. complete, and
    c. balanced.

Advanced Summary Writing

Advanced language proficiency students can actually study summary writing. For example, the (often very brief) instructions for writing summaries usually contain at least three major pieces of vague or even incorrect information:

1. Most definitions of summary writing state that it is "a brief restatement of just the author's main ideas," but an academic summary is much more complex than that.
   a. An effective summary is dependent on the ability of the writer to distinguish main ideas ("general") from details ("specifics").
   b. The length of a summary and whether or not it contains specific detail depends at least on
      (1) the assignment (how long, in comparison with the length of the material to be summarized?)
      (2) the audience (have the readers already read the materials?)
2. Although most instructions to write U.S. academic summaries advise student writers to "use their own words," that is not the case. In the following exercise:
   a. Student writers use the same words for the "main idea" words as the authors did in order to be precise (**boldfaced**).
   b. Student writers use closely related synonyms for some of the words (*italics*).

Notice in the Power Grammar section that follows that students are given specific instruction in the grammar and vocabulary of summary writing.

Sample Exercise

Analyze a Summary[4]

Following is an original text and a summary of that text. As you read both, review summary conventions by reading the comments in the margin. Then, with a partner, complete the questions that follow.

Original text:

One characteristic of effective learning is the area of discussion among classmates. Such interaction is potentially an ideal place for students to form a learning community, but instructors should not assume that all students will participate or learn from this form of collaboration, particularly in online courses. Our recent **research** *demonstrated* that student progress in **economics** *classes result* in better performance by classroom students than by **online students.** The **research** *indicates* that the differences were due to *access* to the **instructor** and to *cooperation* with *fellow students* in **classroom** courses, facets that are unavailable to online students.

Source: Chizmar, J. F., & Walbert, M. S. (1999). Web-based learning environment guided by principles of good teaching practice. *Journal of Economic Education, 30,* 3, 248–250. Retrieved November 11, 2004, from http://www.indiana .edu/~econed/pdffiles/Summer99/chizmar.pdf.

> The text begins with a topic sentence.

> "Our" indicates that this text is a paragraph from an article reporting the authors' research.

> Quotation marks are not used because this paragraph is the original text.

Summary:

Research by Chizmar and Walbert (1999) *showed* that **students** in **classroom**-*based* **economics** *courses achieved* more than **online students** in the same course. The research *revealed* that e-students had less *interaction* with the **instructor** and fewer opportunities to *collaborate* with *classmates.*

> The summary begins by stating the authors and main idea of the article.
> Only main ideas and essential supporting details are included.

1. Count the number of words in each paragraph: original source _____ , summary _____ . How much briefer is the summary?
2. Circle the main ideas and important details in the original text. Draw lines to connect them to the ideas in the summary. If the ideas are not included in the summary, write a question mark (?) next to the ideas in the original text.
3. Are any main ideas in the original materials missing in the summary? Explain your opinion.
4. Are any important supporting details missing in the summary? Explain your opinion.
5. How does the summary fulfill (or not fulfill) the conventions of summary writing listed previously?[5]

The Grammar of Summaries

Few textbook instructions for summary writing discuss the grammar of summaries, but that is necessary, especially for ESL EAP students. The editors and authors of the Houghton Mifflin series *English for Success (EAS)* identified grammar and sentence structures used in authentic academic writing assignments based on published corpus research,[6] and conference presentations.[7] For example, the academic grammar structures particular to summaries were identified and presented so that students could learn those structures as they wrote their summary assignments.[8] In the EAS series, these structures are labeled "Power Grammar."

POWER GRAMMAR

Using the Grammar and Punctuation of Summary Writing

You should use certain grammar and punctuation structures when you write effective summaries. The following illustrates some of those structures.

1. Chiraz (2005) *described* the necessity of using the discussion board at least once a week.

   Use reporting verbs (or other attribution signals) and past tense verbs.

   In the conclusion of the report, Gray (2004) *predicted* that online instructors will add advances in technology to their courses.

   The results of Johnson's research (2005) *indicate* that one major drawback of online discussion boards is their asynchronicity.

   However, use present tense reporting verbs when presenting research results or when reporting "general truth."

2. | Instead of | Use |
   |---|---|
   | *achieved* | *succeeded* |
   | *collaborate* | *cooperate* |
   | *e-students* | *online students* |

   Use synonyms for words when possible.

3. <u>Time</u>: first, second, then
   <u>Addition</u>: furthermore, in addition, additionally
   <u>Result/effect</u>: therefore, for this reason
   <u>Cause</u>: because, as, since
   <u>Emphasis</u>: in fact, indeed
   <u>Example</u>: for instance, as an illustration

   Use logical organizers to help the readers move from one idea to the next. Some categories and example logical organizers are provided. See Appendix 3 for a more extensive list.

4. In Wyman's article "The Power of Your Personal Learning Style," the author states that . . . (2003).

   Within your essay, use correct capitalization and punctuation for titles of original materials:

   The research of online instructor Glenn Merrick (2005) is reported in his book, *Teaching, Learning, and Technology.*

   • The titles of journal, Internet, or newspaper articles written in an essay are put in quotation marks, and all major words* are capitalized.

Seven Principles for Good Practice in Undergraduate Education

Journal of Economic Education

The Online Future

• The titles of books and newspapers written in an essay are italicized or underlined, and all major words* are capitalized.

*Prepositions (*with, by*), articles (*an, the*), and conjunctions (*and, but*) are not capitalized unless they appear as the first word of the title.

5. End-of-Text Citation:

Wyman, P. (2003, June 6). The power of your personal learning style. *How to learn.* Retrieved April 29, 2004, from http://www.howtolearn.com/personal.html

Use correct APA in-text and end-of-text citations.
• See APA in-text citations in the previous examples. Also see Appendix 1.
• Notice the differences between capitalization of titles written in the essay and on the reference page. For more information about end-of-text references, see Appendix 2.
• Notice how end-of-text references are indented and double-spaced.

NOTE: For further explanation of "Power Grammar," see Chapter 18.

Endnotes

1. Tunceren, L. L., & Cavusgil, S. (2006). *College writing 4.* Boston: Houghton Mifflin.
2. Walsh, K. (2006). *College writing 1.* Boston: Houghton Mifflin.
3. Nuttall, G. (2006). *College writing 3.* Boston: Houghton Mifflin.
4. Tunceren & Cavusgil (2006).
5. Tunceren & Cavusgil (2006).
6. See, for example:

   Biber, D., Conrad, S., Reppen, R., Byrd, P., Helt, M., Clark, V. et al. (2004). *Representing language in the university: Analysis of the TOEFL 2000 spoken and written academic language.* ETS TOEFL Monograph Services MS-25. Princeton, NJ: Educational Testing Service.

   Biber, D., Conrad, S., Reppen, R., Byrd, P., & Helt, M. (2002). Speaking and writing in the university: A multidimensional comparison. *TESOL Quarterly 36*(1), 9–48.

   Canseco, G., & Byrd, P. (1989). The writing required of graduate students in business administration. *TESOL Quarterly 23*(2), 305–316.
7. Byrd, P., Schuemann, C., & Reid, J. (2002, April). *Materials behind closed doors: A report on a national survey of ESL teachers in community colleges.* Paper presented at the International TESOL Convention. Salt Lake City.
8. For more specific information about integrating grammar structures with student writing, see Dana Ferris's groundbreaking book, *Treatment of Error in Second Language Writing* (2002). Ann Arbor: University of Michigan Press.

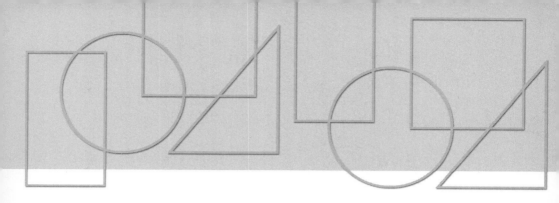

Developing and Assigning Writing Tasks

Academic writing differs from many other types of writing in at least three ways:

1. It is not voluntary.
2 The topic is usually assigned (writers do not usually choose their topics although they sometimes choose a single topic from a list).
3. It is not just read; like any test, it is evaluated.

Designing Writing Assignments

The effects of an academic writing assignment are (a) to measure student skills and (b) to provide a learning opportunity for the writers. That is, students "write to learn" as well as to show what they have already learned about academic writing in class. Successful writing assignments will (a) fulfill the expectations of the teacher-evaluator and at the same time (b) offer students the fairest possible way to demonstrate their writing strengths.

To provide students with the best possible opportunities to demonstrate their writing competence, designers of writing assignments (usually the instructors) must carefully consider the purpose(s), the

parameters, the constraints, and the evaluation criteria for each
assignment. And, just as important, they must clearly communicate those
purposes, parameters, constraints, and criteria to their students.

Consequently, EAP writing teachers are responsible for designing
authentic, relevant writing assignments that motivate and interest students;
that result in transparent, success-building tasks; and that sequence and
spiral the skills and strategies being taught. Easier said than done.

Of course, writing assignments for individual classes may not need the
detail or absolute clarity of large-scale testing because the designer/
assigner is immediately available for questions. The more transparent the
writing assignment, however, the more effectively students will be able to
understand and complete the task.

To prepare students for effective written responses to academic
assignments, the goal for the EAP writing teacher is to teach students
appropriate writing strategies that will allow them to analyze assignments,
gather materials, and present ideas in culturally appropriate forms. Here
are guidelines for developing effective writing assignments.

Assignment Design Guidelines[1]

Context
- Place of writing task in course objectives, curriculum, long-term
  program goals, barrier examinations
- Student capabilities, limitations, learning objectives
- Criteria/reasons for the assignment
- Authentic/real-life situation

Content
- Accessible to all student writers, culturally and otherwise
- Authentic audience and purpose(s)
- Appropriately "rich" (e.g., to allow for multiple approaches)

Language
- Instructions
    Comprehensible
    As brief as clarity allows
    Unambiguous

- Assignment
   Vocabulary and syntax appropriately simple or complex
   Transparent
   Easy to interpret

Task(s)

- Focuses appropriately on accomplishment within external parameters (e.g., time constraints)
- Furthers students' knowledge of classroom content and skills
- Allows students to "demonstrate" their knowledge
- Engages, interests, involves the students

Rhetorical Specifications

- Clear directions concerning shape and format(s)
- Instructions concern register and tone; that is, achieving the appropriate relationship with reader(s)—audience
- Adequate rhetorical cues (i.e., coherence and cohesion cues)

Evaluation (See chapters in Part 4 for a full discussion of evaluation)

- Assesses what is being taught
- Articulates clear, specific, unambiguous criteria to student writers

Sample Successful EAP Writing Assignments (Various Levels of Language Proficiency)

The following sample writing assignments have been designed, assigned, and evaluated by effective instructors. They have also been assessed, revised, and class-tested by those instructors. In each case, students were able to write effective papers from these assignments. Each assignment is preceded by background information to help contextualize the task.

Successful Assignment Example 1

Background: Low Intermediate, U.S. resident/immigrant students, EAP, preparing for entrance to community college; students learn to write academic paragraphs.
Timeline: Chapter 2 (week three to four of a sixteen-week semester)

Sequential Paragraph Assignment[2]

1. Write one paragraph describing <u>either</u> (a) your chosen major field of study <u>or</u> (b) your future occupation. Use the writing process you have practiced in other chapters: Gather Information, Organize and Focus, Revise and Edit.
2. Write a paragraph explaining how an occupation fits OR does not fit a specific person's personality. Use the three-step process you practiced earlier in this chapter to prepare for and write your paragraph.

   To complete this assignment:
   - Gather information about personality characteristics from the Internet
   - Interview a person about (a) his or her career/job and (b) his or her personality characteristics.
   - Analyze the "fit" between the person's occupation and his or her personality
   - Write a report paragraph that states your opinion and supports your opinion with the information you gathered

Successful Assignment Example 2

<u>Background</u>: Low Intermediate, U.S. resident/immigrant students, EAP, preparing for entrance to community college; students learn to write academic paragraphs.
<u>Timeline</u>: Chapter 5: (weeks twelve to fourteen of a sixteen-week semester)

Chapter Assignment[3]

1. Prewriting, building schema
   With a small group of classmates, list features of your college that students would like to see changed. For example, perhaps the library is not open on weekends, or the cafeteria does not offer any vegetarian selections, or not enough sections of required classes are offered in the evenings, or loud conversations among students in hallways disturb classes.
2. Next, discuss each item from the following perspectives:
   a. How many people are affected?
   b. How harmful is the issue to students' academics?
   c. How annoying is it?
   d. How difficult would it be to improve the situation?

3. Assignment
   Choose an issue you are personally interested in seeing changed.
   Because this issue will be the basis for all the writing you will do in this
   chapter, be sure you really are interested in it. You will enjoy the chapter
   far more if you are truly interested in the topic you are writing about.
4. Multiparagraphs in the Assignment
   This is a multiparagraph assignment on one topic, the issue you have
   chosen. Write:
   a. One paragraph that describes the issue and why you think it is
      important. The readers for this topic will be your instructor and
      the members of your class.
   b. One paragraph that offers suggestions for improving the situation.
      The readers for this paragraph will be students at the college,
      whom you will address through your student newspaper.
   c. One paragraph that solicits help from the top administrator at your
      college/campus. The audience for this paragraph will be the
      administrator.

Successful Assignment Example 3

Background: High Intermediate, U.S. resident/immigrant students, EAP
students preparing for entrance to community college; students learn to
write expository essays.
Timeline: Chapter 1: (weeks two to three of a sixteen-week semester)

Multiple-Paragraph Writing Assignments for Review of Body Paragraph Writing[4]

Writing Assignment 1

*Follow the three steps of the writing process (gathering information, focusing
and organizing, revising and editing) to write a paragraph that describes the
ways one of the ads on the previous page attracts consumers.*

Focus of the Assignment: Method of Development:
describe the ways   *classification*

Gather some information for this paragraph with a small group of classmates who chose the same ad. Then write the paragraph by yourself.

Keep all the materials, drafts, and peer reviews for this assignment in a writing folder. Later in the chapter, you will be asked to turn in your folder to your instructor.

Writing Assignment 2

Choose one of the two ads below. Follow the three steps of the writing process to write a paragraph in which you describe two or three marketing stimuli used that result in an effective ad.

Focus of the Assignment: Method of Development:
effects of the stimuli   *effects*

Keep all the materials for this writing assignment in your writing folder. Your instructor will collect your writing folder when you finish the assignment.

Writing Assignment 3

Write a paragraph in which you compare and contrast two or three major stimuli used in the two ads. Decide which ad is more effective than the other.

Focus of the Assignment: Method of Development:
evaluate   *compare/contrast*

Use the three-step writing process to develop and organize the ideas for your paragraph. Keep all the materials you develop for this writing assignment in a writing folder. You will turn in your writing folder to your instructor after you finish the assignment.

Successful Assignment Example 4

<u>Background</u>: High Intermediate, U.S. resident/immigrant students, EAP students preparing for entrance to community college; students learn to write expository essays.

<u>Timeline</u>: Chapter 3 (weeks six to seven of a sixteen-week semester)

Chapter 3 Essay Assignment[5]

In each of the following topics, a person has been partially deprived of one of her or his senses. Select one of the assignments to research and report about. For this research report, investigate the topic on the Internet.

1. A person whose vision is impaired has decided to have Lasix surgery. In a three-page research report, write:
   a. A background paragraph that describes how vision can become impaired; use a diagram to show the biology of impaired vision
   b. Two to four body paragraphs discussing the advantages and disadvantages of Lasix surgery

2. What happens when a person loses her or his sense of taste? Select one reason a person may partially or completely lose the sense of taste. Write a three-page research report that includes:
   a. A background paragraph describing ONE reason why a person could lose part or all of the sense of taste; use a diagram to show how that happens
   b. Two to four body paragraphs that
      (1) discuss the short-term and/or the long-term effect(s) of losing all or part of one's sense of taste (for your selected reason)
      (2) explain way(s) of restoring or improving one's sense of taste

3. A person who is hard of hearing can often be helped by a hearing aid. Select one way a person may become hard of hearing and need to use a hearing aid. In a three-page research report, write:
   a. A background paragraph that explains ONE way a person can become hard of hearing; use a diagram to show what happens when a person loses some of her or his hearing
   b. Two to four body paragraphs discussing the process used by (digital) hearing aids to help a person who is hard of hearing

To complete this assignment, you need to:

1. Complete an Internet search
2. Write a report by following the three-step writing process you learned in previous chapters

Your essay must include:

- an introductory paragraph
- a background paragraph
- two or three additional body paragraphs
- one or two in-text references
- a concluding paragraph
- a reference page at the end of the paper

Successful Assignment Example 5

Background: Advanced, U.S. resident/immigrant students, EAP students preparing for entrance to community college; students learn to write academic essays/reports.

Timeline: Chapter 2 (weeks four to five of a sixteen-week semester)

Chapter 2 Writing Assignment[6]

Choose a disease to research.

1. Gather information about the disease.
2. Summarize, paraphrase, and quote relevant material.
3. Draft a background paragraph.
4. Draft body paragraphs, each developed according to its purpose.
5. Draft the introduction and concluding paragraphs.
6. Include in-text citation and a reference page in APA style.
7. Revise and edit the essay.

Unsuccessful Writing Assignments from across the Curriculum

The following authentic assignments, collected from a variety of U.S. college/university classes, were poorly designed, so they caused difficulties for students in the classes. Notice:

1. Each assignment is preceded by:
   a. A summary evaluation of the problems in the assignment
   b. Some background information about the discipline from which the assignment originated
2. Each assignment is followed by questions and confusions reported by the students

Unsuccessful Assignment Example 1

Evaluation: The most frequent problem is that the assignment is too broadly focused: the content is so inclusive that students cannot fulfill the expectations of the teacher-evaluator within the constraints of the assignment.

Background: First-year undergraduate Music Appreciation class

Timeline: First assignment (second week of a sixteen-week semester)

Write a three- to five-page research paper on a musical topic. The purpose of this assignment is to familiarize you with music resources in the library. You must cite in your paper at least three different sources found in the library. This paper must be typed and double-spaced. The paper is worth a maximum of sixty points.

Students' questions involved the expectations about the topic: What is a musical topic—rap? use of the violin on Broadway? classical music? how Bach's life affected his composing? Elvis?

Unsuccessful Assignment Example 2

Evaluation: Sometimes the assignment is flawed in terms of **context**: that is, the assignment is not clear about how it relates to the course, what the capabilities of the students are, and what the students will learn.

> NOTE: In the example below, the content is also flawed; students are directed to provide information about so many broad topics that their seven- to ten-page paper will almost certainly be much longer.

Background: Second-year undergraduate History of Science class (for nonmajors)

Timeline: Just before midterm of a sixteen-week semester

Write a seven- to ten-page paper with at least seven different sources on the (1) social, (2) political, (3) philosophical, and (4) religious consequences of Darwinism. This paper should place Darwin's theory in its (5) cultural context, examining Western culture (6) before, (7) during, and (8) after Origin of Species. *(9) How did people react to the theory? (10) Why did they react to it? [numbers of tasks added]*

Students' questions involved (a) why such a huge paper had been assigned about a topic they had spent just a week on during class, (b) their disgust discovering that the paper was worth almost nothing in their overall class grade, a piece of information not given to them until after the papers were returned to them.

Unsuccessful Assignment Example 3

<u>Evaluation</u>: Still other assignments have inaccurate or incomprehensible language.
<u>Background</u>: Second-year undergraduate economics class
<u>Timeline</u>: Final paper, assigned early in the semester, due at the end of the sixteen-week semester

Within a lengthy assignment, the ambiguity of this sentence frustrated many students:

> The paper should be chosen in consultation with the instructor with a rough outline submitted by the 10th week of the course.

<u>Students questioned</u> whether (and many assumed that) they should wait until the tenth week of class to meet and discuss a topic with the instructor.

Guidelines for Analysis of Writing Assignments

Is the context of the assignment
_____ irrelevant to the course and/or to the students?
_____ unreasonable, considering the students' capabilities and learning objectives?

Is the content of the assignment
_____ too broad to be accomplished within the assignment parameters?
_____ outside the expertise, experience, or researchability of the student writers?

Is the language of the instructions or the assignment
_____ too simple or too complex?
_____ culturally biased?
_____ too abstract or philosophical?
_____ unacademic or otherwise inappropriate?

Are the students' responses to the assignment
____ trite?
____ highly emotional?
____ similar to each other?
____ misleading or confusing?

NOTE: Parts of this chapter were adapted from an article by Reid and Kroll, 1995.

Endnotes

1. Reid, J., & Kroll, B. (1995). Designing and assessing effective classroom writing assignments for NES and ESL students. *Journal of Second Language Writing, 4*(1), 17–41.
2. Cotter, E. (2006). *College writing 2.* Boston: Houghton Mifflin.
3. Nuttall, G. (2006). *College writing 3.* Boston: Houghton Mifflin.
4. Tunceren, L. L., & Cavusgil, S. (2006). *College writing 4.* Boston: Houghton Mifflin.
5. Tunceren, L. L., & Cavusgil, S. (2006). *College writing 4.* Boston: Houghton Mifflin.
6. Tunceren, L. L., & Cavusgil, S. (2006). *College writing 4.* Boston: Houghton Mifflin.

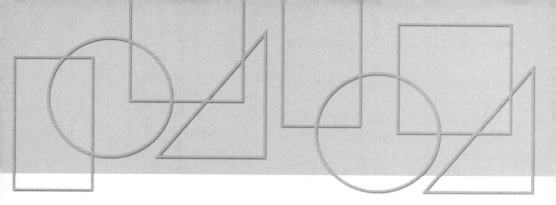

Chapter **11**

Teaching ESL EAP Students Research Strategies

Most experienced ESL writing teachers find that students have difficulty learning three major writing skills:

1. The concept and importance of an audience, of readers outside the student writer
2. The concept and successful use of general and specific (see Chapter 10)
3. The concepts and multiple uses of citation/references

In each case, these skills must be spiraled into increasingly difficult learning scenarios throughout a writing program. The first two are dealt with in prior chapters. In this chapter, the focus is on research strategies, use of library resources, and particularly the use of the World Wide Web (WWW) and the Internet.

Assumptions about Students, Academic Research, and Citation

1. Students know they do not know enough about citation and referencing.
2. Most students want to do good research and cite sources appropriately.

3. Many students plagiarize **not** because they choose to fool the teacher, but because:
   a. They do not know enough about citation and referencing
   b. They believe that the original author sounds better than they ever could
   c. They are panicked by the need to do acceptable research
4. Students who plagiarize deliberately need to (a) be given the opportunity to learn about citation and referencing and (b) be ready to accept the institutional consequences.
5. Most undergraduate college writing assignments require students to do research.
6. Because students take courses in many disciplines, they need strategies to:
   a. Analyze a writing assignment (purpose, audience, and processes that will fulfill the expectations of the academic reader)
   b. Do appropriate, adequate research, using
      (1) themselves as the "researcher" (the student writer): through observation, memory, prior experiences
      (2) library resources, including books, journals, maps, other media
      (3) the WWW, including URLs, search engines, webpages, and other materials
      (4) interviews and surveys of others (firsthand research)
      (5) correct in-text citations and end-of-text references for sources

NOTE: Many students prefer to use only the Internet for any college research they do. You will have to decide whether your students should expand their research knowledge and work to include the college library, interviews, or other resources.

Plagiarism

Problems with citation and plagiarism can be solved by starting research strategies early and then spiraling discussions and learning experiences throughout the writing program.

Explanation

Plagiarism is a frequent and usually serious problem for ESL writers. Even if you have explained the rules for citation, those rules can get lost between the head and the hand, perhaps because students (a) cannot imagine writing "better" than (or even as clearly as) the source of their information or (b) do not know enough about the topic to change the words appropriately or (c) are hurried, harried, and panic-stricken. Whatever the reasons, the process of beginning citation use early, using an incremental approach and continually spiraling the use of citation in increasingly sophisticated contexts, provides students with adequate time and practice to become more self-confident and knowledgeable about using the ideas and/or the words of authorities.

NOTE: See additional discussion of plagiarism later in this chapter.

<u>The single rule for what/who to cite</u>: **Whatever information you did not know when you began this writing assignment must be cited (a) in the text and (b) on the end-of-text reference list.**

Teachers cope with the problems of plagiarism by beginning with simple concepts and references. They begin with lower-proficiency-level students, explaining the importance of "research" writing, helping students prepare for more academic writing tasks, and then spiraling the use of research and writing through higher levels.

1. Less proficient, even basic writing students are capable of:
   a. Collecting and reporting personal data (e.g., personal experiences)
   b. Reporting the results of short surveys
   c. Interviewing family members and reporting the results of those interviews
   d. Using research vocabulary, such as "data collection" and "research report"
2. Students with intermediate language proficiency can:
   a. Learn about and practice one citation style format
   b. Look at ways other writers use both in-text and end-of-text citations
   c. Use the Internet and learn to
      (1) cite one to three sources in their paragraphs and essays (in-text citations)
      (2) write a short reference page (one to three sources) at the end of their assignments (end-of-text citations)

3. Advanced ESL writers are able to:
   a. Design their own surveys and interviews, as well as carry them out and report their results
   b. Evaluate the credibility of websites as they use the Internet
   c. Use library resources, including books and journal articles, newspapers, and other media
   d. Work with a variety of attribution structures
   e. Use multiple references

Because advanced students may have been investigating and practicing research strategies for an extended period of time, they usually feel more comfortable with online research assignments. But only with additional encouragement and practice will they become effective library researchers.

Having students collect authentic data in the form of interviews and surveys can serve as a valuable introduction to research strategies at all proficiency levels. Their findings are real and concrete.

Using Interviews and Surveys

- Interviews versus surveys
- Interviewing authoritative sources
- Guidelines for interviews
- Designing and using surveys
- Guidelines for survey design

Teaching Suggestions

Ask students to give reasons for citing sources. It is important that they go beyond the single answer: plagiarism. Usually students can fully understand and appreciate the reasons for citation, but only if they know about them.

1. The legal (and cultural) reason: to give credit to the original author (or speaker) where the students found the information. In U.S. academic culture, not to give credit is to commit **plagiarism** (using the ideas of someone else as your own).
2. The social reasons:
   a. As a courtesy to readers, writers give exact citations. That way, interested readers can find each source easily.

    b. Citing sources lends credibility to a student writer's ideas/opinions, especially when an authority agrees with the student writer. Readers appreciate and are more easily persuaded by the strength of such sources.

  3. The political reason: Using a variety of credible sources demonstrates to the instructor/evaluator of the paper that the student writer is capable of researching a topic and giving credit to each research source. Citing sources is therefore beneficial in the testing processes of academic writing. It impresses the instructor/evaluator.

APA Citation

APA (American Psychological Association) citation format is widely used in undergraduate courses across the curriculum. Whether you use APA or another citation form, students need to understand that different academic disciplines use different but equally specific citation formats and that learning the basics of one form will give them a solid foundation for analyzing and using other formats effectively.

    Remember that all referencing formats, including APA style, are in flux, especially regarding Internet sequencing and documentation in end-of-text citations. Therefore, check the APA website (and/or have students do the same) each semester. Here is the APA website URL: http//:www.apa.org.

> NOTE: MLA citation format is favored by English teachers, but it is used only rarely outside the English Department.

Teaching Suggestion

Encourage students to practice "lead-ins" and reporting verbs like the following to introduce source information and to distinguish carefully between the author of the resource and the student writers' ideas/opinions. In the examples below, the boldfaced **Last** indicates the last name of the author.

1. In a recent study, **Last** (2005) states that . . .
2. Results of a recent study (**Last** & **Last**, 2004) suggest that . . .
3. First **Last** [*or* **Last**], in her recent study of X, demonstrated that . . . (2005).

4. According to **Last** (2005), "The use of irradiation in foods . . . destroys thyroid hormones" (p. XX).
5. In a series of recent experiments, **Last** has <u>found</u> that "reflexology has made many . . important discoveries . . ." (2005, p. XXX).

Here is a list of "**reporting verbs**." Notice:

1. Most are followed by "that."
2. Some are "stronger" (e.g., *stated, demonstrated*) than others (*claimed, suggested*).
3. Students need to base their verb choices on the context: Is the information suggesting or arguing? Did the researcher claim or assert?

explained	presented	examined	described	discussed
maintained	examined	revealed	contended	alleged
implied	proposed	argued	assumed	indicated
suggested	stated	noted	showed	demonstrated
reported	observed	investigated	predicted	recommended
found	claimed	asserted	revealed	hypothesized

Each time students begin research for a new writing assignment, you may need to remind them:

1. The purposes of citing the words and ideas of others are:
   a. To support the student writer's ideas and opinions with the ideas of authorities
   b. To give credit to the original author
2. They should be careful to represent the materials of authorities objectively. For example, they should not take a single sentence that seems to support one of their ideas (e.g., a paragraph, an article) if the author actually disagrees with their idea.

You will probably also need to review and stress the problems with plagiarism each time students begin to research a writing assignment. Remind them that many U.S. academic readers view plagiarism very harshly, so students must learn to fulfill their instructors' expectations in the use of citations. Following is a possible handout to clarify problems with plagiarism that students, both native English speakers and ESL students, frequently encounter.

PLAGIARISM HANDOUT[1]

Example Sentence: Plagiarism is not only illegal; it is unethical and often just plain lazy.

1. Full quotation: According to Shelley Reid (2005), "Plagiarism is not only illegal; it is unethical and often just plain lazy" (p. 26).
   - The author is mentioned in the sentence (so not included in the citation).
   - The author's full name is included the first time she or he is mentioned.
   - The author's name is followed by the year of publication in parentheses.
   - A comma follows the introduction of the direct quotation.
   - The first word of the quotation is capitalized.
   - Closing quotation marks follow the direct quotation.
   - The page number of the quotation follows quotation marks in parentheses.
   - A period completes the sentence after the page number in parentheses.
2. Partial quotation with paraphrase of general ideas: Plagiarism, says Reid (2005), as well as being illegal, is "unethical and often just plain lazy" (p. 26).
   - The author is mentioned in the sentence by last name only because her full name was used in the first citation.
   - A comma is not included before a partial quotation that fits into the sentence.
   - A partial quotation does not begin with a capital letter.
3. Partial quotation with ellipsis (three dots separated by spaces): Some people argue that "plagiarism is . . . unethical and just plain lazy" (Reid, 2005, p. 26).
   - The author's name is not mentioned in the sentence, so it is included in the parenthetical citation.
   - A comma is not included.
   - It does not begin with a capital letter (the quotation begins in the middle of the sentence).
   - Ellipsis: three dots separated by spaces [plural: ellip**ses**] are used to indicate that some words have been left out of the original author's quotation.

4. Original paraphrase of the author's ideas: It has been argued that plagiarism demonstrates laziness as well as being legally and ethically wrong (Reid, 2005).
   - The author's name is not mentioned in the sentence, so it is included in the citation.
   - No page number is required in the citation because there is no direct quotation; however, you may include the page number if you choose.
5. Known fact: Plagiarism is illegal.
   - No citation is needed because readers generally know this fact.

Teaching Suggestion

I tell my students that if they are not certain about the "parts" of end-of-text citation, the first and most important step is to <u>be consistent</u>. For instance, put the year in the same place in each citation, and capitalize and punctuate using the same rules throughout. Paying attention to the small details is crucial; at the very least, if students are consistent they can then explain to academic instructors that the form they used is what they learned previously (☺).

Academic Research

It is probably a good idea to informally survey your students about their previous uses of research. Following are the major tasks students need to perform in a library.

1. You may find that most students have used reference works in the library to find information about a topic in such texts as:
   a. A general encyclopedia, like the *Encyclopedia American*
   b. A more field-specific encyclopedia, such as the *Encyclopedia of Thermodynamics*
   c. A general dictionary or a field-specific dictionary

   If your students do not have this experience, a reference librarian can direct students to these basic reference materials.

2. Many students may have also had experiences looking for books in a library. If not, you might discuss the following tasks:
   a. Locating books about the topic by searching the online catalog (in the library or from their own computers—at home!)

  (1) Typing keywords about the topic

  (2) Discovering the call numbers of books

  (3) Studying a library map to discover where those call numbers are located

  (4) Finding the location and the book

  (5) Quickly skimming the table of contents and perhaps the index to see whether or not the information is related to their topic

  (6) Photocopying pages or checking out relevant books

3. As more and more magazine/journal articles become available online, students may never have been taught (and then successfully searched for) articles in the library. If you choose to teach students this process, remember that they might find this task unnecessarily difficult, when compared with the online articles.

 a. Locating magazines (journals) by searching an online browser or database (in the library or from another computer—even their own, from home!)

  (1) Typing key words about the topic

  (2) Discovering articles in magazines (journals) about the topic

  (3) Finding out whether each article is

   (a) on the WWW and accessible to the student (or not)

    • Locating the article

    • Skimming it to see if it contains related information

    • Printing relevant articles

   (b) in the library and accessible to the student (or not)

    • Locating the article by discovering the call number of the magazine

     — If the article is current, proceeding to the current periodical shelves in the library and locating the article

      ◦ Skimming it to see if it contains related information

      ◦ Photocopying relevant articles

    • If the article is older, proceeding to the location of the call number (in the library), locating

     — That number

     — The correct volume (by year)

     — The article

      ◦ Skimming it to see if it contains related information and photocopying relevant articles

NOTE: While planning for the research tasks in your course, schedule a tour of the library or provide library contact information in your syllabus.

Using the Internet

Despite the wealth of information available in academic libraries, some students will continue to be too intimidated—or frustrated by prior library experiences—to use those resources. Instead, they will choose to use sources on the Web. For that reason, the major focus of this section is on using the Internet for research purposes.

> NOTE: This is a difficult section to write because it's hard to judge your knowledge about the World Wide Web (WWW) and the Internet. So, to begin, for a more complete explanation of the Internet, see *Essentials for Reading* in this series. The authors, Sharon Seymour and Laura Walsh, provide complete, accessible information about using the Internet.[2] Instead of repeating that information here, this section focuses on using the Internet for **Writing** research.

The Basics of Using the Internet for Research

Most students beginning research on the Web will use a browser (such as Google) and choose three to six keywords that describe their specific topic. Effective strategies for selecting keywords include these:

1. Use nouns whenever possible: airbags + children + injury + death.
2. Put the most important words first: Japan + censorship + movies + films + books.
3. Put a plus (+) before any word to be included in the search: cost + advertisements + television + minute.
4. Put a minus (−) before any word to be excluded from search: scent + fragrance flowers + insects − animals + nasturtiums.
5. Use phrases instead of single words, and put quotation marks around those phrases: "Hong Kong" + "tourist shopping" + entertainment + restaurants + discos.

Other strategies for effectively searching the Web that students should understand include these:

1. Become an expert on one search engine (my suggestion is Google) by reading the "Help" files.
2. Always recheck spelling of keywords and URLs.

   NOTE: Web addresses, called Universal Resource Locators (URLs), recognize both capital and lowercase letters, so be sure to type the address with the correct capital and lowercase letters.

3. Learn to refine (i.e., narrow further) the results of a topic search.
4. Be patient and flexible; search engines are not perfect.
5. Understand that the WWW does not contain all knowledge.

The result of selecting effective keywords is usually a list of documents on the Web about the topic and the URLs of those websites. Clicking on any document title will access the information. Students should know or be taught that if the list is too long (more than fifty sources), adding descriptors will further focus the search. If the list is too short (fewer than ten), subtract one of the keywords.

Citing WWW Material

For WWW material, the APA in-text citation remains the same as for sources found in the library: (**Last**, year). For end-of-text citation (a separate reference page at the end of the paper), students list complete citations alphabetically by the authors' last names. The general APA form for WWW references is:

Last, F. (Day Month Year of Publication or Placement of the Materials on the WWW). *Title of document*. Retrieved Month Day, Year you accessed the material: [type complete URL without a period at the end]

NOTE: Remember:

The APA Internet site for citations is http//:www.bk.psu.edu/academic/library/APAStyle.html.

Teaching Non-Text Materials

Although most academic writing is primarily text, non-text materials are often an integral part of academic writing assignments, particularly in science, technology, and business. Students need to be able to integrate charts and tables into their writing assignments when appropriate.

Teaching Non-Text Materials

- Using non-text materials
- Writing conventions for non-text materials
- Citing non-text materials

Endnotes

1. My thanks to Shelley Reid, Director of Composition at George Mason University, for this handout.
2. Seymour, S., & Walsh, L. (2006). *Essentials for teaching academic reading*. Boston: Houghton Mifflin.

Part **4**

Responding to and Evaluating Student Writing

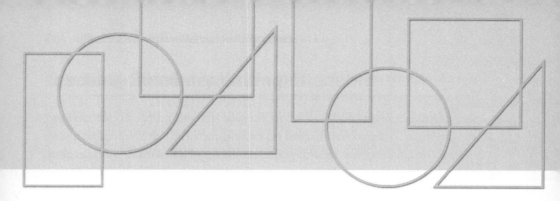

12

Opportunities for Feedback on Student Writing

Student Responsibility for Feedback

Before students turn in a draft of their writing for teacher response, they need to understand:

1. The teacher is only one of several people who should respond.
2. The students have the responsibility to seek feedback from others before they request teacher response.

The first respondent is the student himself or herself, and writer-responders need the skills and strategies to look carefully at their own writing frequently and closely. They might, for instance:

1. Reread their drafts two or three times, thereby rebuilding lost momentum
2. Read their draft aloud and "listen" for language problems
3. Reflect on a draft without the paper in hand, in "empty moments" (e.g., washing dishes, walking to class), considering possible changes

Textbook Exercises: Revision

Following are examples of activities that students can use to learn about and practice revising strategies. Each series of exercises on the next pages is arranged by student English language proficiency. Exercises below focus on high-advanced learners; the next page contains exercises for intermediate students; the last page has exercises for more advanced learners. Students can work with student sample texts in their books or with exercises that focus on their own writing. Each of these exercises can be completed individually or with a partner or with a small group of peers.

Example 1

Using a Student Sample

Anxiety before a test is always there because I cannot predict anything about my test, and it makes me very thoughtful about what the exam or question will be like because the phase of anticipation is very hard, but at the time of the exam, every hidden idea is revealed and no more anxiety is left except for timing, so in order to control my anxiety, to be more confident and concentrate and not to think about anything else, I just relax and believe in myself. My advice to any student is to be prepared, study, and learn hard before a test and concentrate at the time of the test.[1]

Labiba

Exercise A: Noticing sentence length

When you were reading Labiba's writing, did you notice how long her first sentence was? Could you say it out loud in a single breath? Would you agree that her sentence is too long? ____ Yes ____ No

Exercise B: Analyzing a long sentence

List the ideas in Labiba's first sentence separately. The first and second ideas have been completed for you. The connecting words are in brackets.

1. <u>Anxiety before a test is always there   </u> / [because]
2. <u>I cannot predict anything about my test</u> / [and]
3. _____ / [because]
4. _____ / [but]
5. _____ / [and]
6. _____ [so]
7. _____ .

Exercise C: Rewriting a long sentence

1. With a partner, divide Labiba's sentences into three or more shorter sentences.
2. With your partner, read Labiba's new sentences aloud.
   a. Are they more comfortable to say?
   b. Do they sound appropriate?
   c. Do they reflect Labiba's ideas?
   d. Compare your revised sentences with another pair of classmates' sentences.
   e. How are the sentences similar?
   f. In what ways are they different?

Example 2

Evaluating Student's Own Writing

Exercise A: Self-checking clauses[2]

Reread your sentences with dependent clauses and check the following:

   a. Did you remember to add the comma if the dependent clause is before the independent clause?
   b. Did you begin each sentence with a capital letter and end it with punctuation?
   c. Did you put *brackets* and *curly brackets* in your Word Bank?

After you have corrected any problems in your sentences, hand your sentences in to your instructor.

Exercise B: Reviewing your letter format

After you have completed your letter, check it carefully against the sample letter. Then answer these questions:

1. Is the date in the correct place?	___ Yes	___ No
2. Is the person's title used (Mr./Mrs./Ms)?	___ Yes	___ No
3. Is there a comma after the name of the person?	___ Yes	___ No
4. Is each paragraph indented?	___ Yes	___ No
5. Is there an appropriate closing (Sincerely, Yours truly,)?	___ Yes	___ No
6. Are the margins correct?	___ Yes	___ No

Exercise C: Editing your letter

Now check your letter for sentence correctness and language level.

1. Highlight or underline each subject and verb.
2. Circle these words: *when, before, after, as soon as, although, because, if.*
3. Circle Yes or No for each question:
   a. Does each clause have a subject and verb?   ____ Yes ____ No
   b. Is each dependent clause attached to an
      independent clause?   ____ Yes ____ No
   c. Does each sentence begin with a capital letter?   ____ Yes ____ No
   d. Does each sentence end with punctuation?   ____ Yes ____ No
   e. Did you use academic language
      (not conversational language)?   ____ Yes ____ No

Exercise D: Reviewing your essay writing[3]

Read your whole essay with a critical eye. Make notes on your essay where you can improve:

1. Coherence: smooth transitions and logical order of ideas
2. Cohesion: repetition of keywords and synonyms; pronouns and articles
3. Unity: relevant points and details only; all information supports the thesis
4. Support: adequate to develop the thesis/topic sentences
5. Sentence variety: different structures and connectors, especially cause-effect
6. Intext citation of sources: (parenthetical references)
7. List of references at the end of the report
8. Mechanics: punctuation, spelling, word forms, verb tenses, and so on

Peer Response

Peers can be an excellent first audience for student writing. Effective peer response can be helpful because peers:

1. Can serve as interested readers for the information in the paper
2. Know the assignment and the "scenario" for writing and so can offer good feedback

3. Are also focusing on the necessary writing strategies and skills to become competent academic writers, so it is in their best interest to be helpful
4. Can help writers better understand the expectations of the instructor
5. Are not evaluating or assigning grades, and so their feedback is nonthreatening
6. May read and comment on drafts in ways that help the writer revise

> NOTE: Of course, the writers should know that, after carefully reviewing the responses of their peers, the writers themselves are responsible for making the final revisions.

Peer response should start early in the writing process and can take place throughout the writing process. Examples:

- Partner/small-group discussion about the assignment
- Partner/small-group responses to topic selection
- Small-group/whole-class responses to narrowed topic
- Ongoing reading and responding by student-writer
- Teacher and/or peer draft responses:
   a. After the first draft
   b. After the second draft, and so on

Teaching Suggestions

Here are some ways to structure pair or group feedback work to use in class.

With a partner or in a small group, students can read other's drafts (or parts of drafts) and then:

1. Write, at the end of the draft, what was most interesting and most memorable.
2. Underline the thesis/topic sentences.
3. Write the essay map for the essay.
4. Complete one or more exercise in the chapter, and then (a) discuss the results with the partner/group and/or (b) report the results to the class.
5. Ask two questions of clarification about the draft (needs prior training/modeling).
6. Write/ask two questions that might help the author improve the draft (needs prior training/modeling).

Issues in Peer Response

For the teacher, the important issue surrounding peer review/evaluation is the students' perception of what they believe about the responsibilities of the teacher versus the students. First, many students believe it is not their job to find and/or correct other students' written errors, to critique or evaluate someone else's paper, or to make suggestions on how to improve a peer's writing. Second, many students have only limited skills in those areas, and most are unwilling to participate fully in judging the quality of peer writing.[4]

They may be right. Each teacher must decide the extent to which the community of writers will become involved in evaluation and correction of peer writing.

> NOTE: I have experimented with various forms of peer work, and presently, while I continue to have students meet in pairs or with small groups of peers throughout the writing process, I do not ask them to correct or judge another student's writing. I do ask them to pair- or group-brainstorm about another student's topic; to put an asterisk in the margin of another student's draft where high-quality/interesting details appear; and to ask one question about another student's paragraph or essay that might help the author.

Teaching Suggestions

Peer response is an excellent way to teach students about reader(s)-audience, to show them how to read closely and make comments and suggestions about a partner's writing, and to build a community of writers. The more structured the peer response exercises, the more focused and helpful the work will be.[5] Even if you decide not to have students evaluate each other's writing, substantial pair and group work in the writing classroom can be both pleasant and helpful for the students. The structure of the tasks can focus on the positive aspects of peer writing: helping a peer select and perhaps narrow a topic, asking partners or peers for advice on a thorny problem, communicating what was most memorable or "best" about a peer's paper.

Below are examples of structured peer response exercises (space for writing has been removed). Notice that the peer response exercises are a kind of "rubric": that is, the teacher sets up certain criteria and asks students to respond with their opinions. Teachers may use the language in these criteria in their assessment rubrics as they respond to and evaluate student writing.

Example 1

<u>Background</u>: Intermediate ESL Writing, third week of the course
<u>Writing Assignment</u>: writing a paragraph

Peer Response[6]

Name of Writer _____

Name of Reader _____ Date _____

Wide Angle View

    Format

        Is the paragraph indented?   Yes/No

        Does the paragraph have one indentation?   Yes/No

        Does the writing go from margin to margin?   Yes/No

    Organization

        Is there a topic sentence?   Yes/No

        Write the topic sentence here: _____

        _____

        How many major points support the topic sentence? _____

        What are they? _____

        _____

        Do supporting details describe the major points?   Yes/No

        Give an example _____

        _____

Close Up View

    Content

        Put an * in the margin of the paragraph next to the information
you found most interesting.

Zoom In On Grammar

        List any adjectives in the paragraph _____

        _____

        List any adjective clauses _____

        _____

        List any verbs that confuse you _____

        _____

Example 2

<u>Background</u>: High-Intermediate to Advanced Students, Week 4 or 5
<u>Assignment</u>: Write an expository essay
Revision Checklist for the Author[7]

*Read the list below very carefully. Check (✓) each item as you **review your essay**. Revise any part of your essay that does not conform to this checklist. When you finish, place this checklist in your writing folder.*

Introduction

____ The essay topic is mentioned in the first sentence of the introduction.
____ The introduction grabs the reader's attention with a description, a dialogue, a surprising fact, a thought-provoking question, or an interesting anecdote.
____ The thesis statement includes the essay's main idea and controlling ideas.

Body Paragraphs

____ Each body paragraph has a topic sentence that states the paragraph's controlling ideas.
____ Keywords and phrases from the thesis statement are used in the topic sentences.
____ The topic sentence controls the main points of each body paragraph.
____ Each body paragraph has clear evidence supporting the main points.
____ Enough relevant details are given to make the evidence easy for readers to understand.
____ The in-text citations follow the correct format shown on page ____.
____ Each body paragraph has a concluding sentence that refers to the paragraph's main idea.

Conclusion

____ The essay has a clear conclusion that summarizes the essay's main idea and main points.
____ The conclusion does not introduce an idea that is not discussed in the body paragraphs.

References Page

　　——　The end-of-text citations follow the correct format shown on
　　　　　page——.
　　——　Appendix

Online Revision (Feedback) Resources

Other potential respondents include on-campus services that help
students. For instance, colleges usually have "writing centers" or "help
centers" where student writers can receive feedback from trained writers.[8]
Usually, students make appointments to meet with writing "tutors" and
discuss their writing.

> NOTE: Students must understand that such help centers are not
> places to "drop off" their drafts and return to "pick up" the
> improved papers. Instead, students discuss their specific writing
> questions; the tutors do not "proofread" or "rewrite" student papers.

Another source of feedback is online college/university writing
laboratories (called OWLs) that allow students to e-mail written drafts.
Tutors at the OWL will then comment on the students' drafts and return
those drafts. In addition, many OWLs have fully developed "resource
centers," pages of the website devoted to rhetorical and grammatical
information that students can access easily.

> NOTE: Many OWLs have stopped accepting student writing from
> students who do not attend that school. Students can still try the
> OWLs at Purdue University (purdue.English.edu) and Colorado State
> University (writing.colostate.edu).

Endnotes

1. Walsh, K. (2006). *College writing 1.* Boston: Houghton Mifflin.
2. Cotter, E. (2006). *College writing 2.* Boston: Houghton Mifflin.
3. Tunceren, L. L., & Cavusgil, S. (2006). *College writing 4.* Boston: Houghton Mifflin.
4. Nelson, G. L., & Carson, J. G. (1998). ESL students' perceptions of effectiveness in peer response groups. *Journal of Second Language Writing, 7,* 113–131.
5. Ferris, D. R., & Hedgcock, J. S. (2005). *Teaching ESL composition: Purpose, process, and practice* (2nd ed.). Mahwah, NJ: Erlbaum.
6. From *College Writing 2* (Cotter, 2006)
7. Nuttall, G. (2006). *College Writing 3.* Boston: Houghton Mifflin.
8. Thonus, T. (2003). Serving generation 1.5 learners in the university writing center. *TESOL Journal, 12,* 17–24.

Chapter **13**

Preparing to Respond to Student Writing

Although teacher evaluation of student writing often includes some teacher response (written or oral comments on the computer or on the students' papers), teacher response can (and should) sometimes occur without evaluation. That is, of the numerous roles that EAP writing teachers assume, the "responder-coach" role can be one of the most effective and most pleasant. This chapter and the next focus on the teacher as responder.[1]

Basic Assumptions about Response

- Responding need not be evaluative, although students often see it in this light.
- Responding is not a single act.
- Teacher response is not the only kind of response a student should receive.
- One major purpose of response is to motivate and encourage students.
- Another purpose is to turn the students back into the writing process.
- Students generally take teacher response very seriously.[2]

Issues in Teacher Response[3]

- What role(s) can/should teachers play in the response process?
- How much should teachers mark?
- Should teachers concentrate on language errors or rhetorical errors?
- How can teachers prepare students to receive response appropriately?
- How can teachers prepare students to benefit from responses?
- Should teachers determine the individual way(s) in which their students prefer and/or benefit from responses?

The answers (or "responses"!) to the previous questions lie in a teacher's philosophy of response. Many differences exist in EAP writing teachers' attitudes about response. For example, some ESL EAP writing teachers (myself included) agree with current research. It suggests that teachers who mark student <u>drafts</u> numerous times may actually be hindering student progress because (a) many students become dependent on teachers' responses and (b) there is substantial opportunity for instructors to "appropriate" their students' ideas and writing (i.e., the students' writing becomes more their teacher's writing).[4]

Yet, research also shows that training students to work again and again with their writing helps their writing skills. Therefore, although you may choose to work with student drafts, particularly at lower levels of student language proficiency, you should still be asking students to take primary responsibility for their own writing.

Teaching Suggestion

Stress that the more prepared student writers are for feedback, the more they may discover that readers' suggestions and opinions can be helpful. That is, the saying "garbage in, garbage out" is relevant for all opportunities for feedback.

1. If writers come unprepared for peer response work, with partially or roughly constructed papers, the response(s) will be less helpful. In contrast, if writers come prepared, with developed papers, specific questions, and openness to the opinions of others, peer response can be especially effective.
2. The same is true for teacher response. The less "prepared" the draft, the more difficult it is for the teacher to respond appropriately (without, for instance, appropriating the paper).

3. When students meet with a writing center tutor, no work will occur unless the writer initiates the meeting with specific questions about the paper.

Approaches to Responding

For less experienced or lower-language-proficient student writers, one way to support student responsibility is to look only at student drafts during a face-to-face encounter with the student writer, either at formal student conferences or with less formal student-teacher conferencing experiences.

Conferencing with Students[5]

Determine whether to hold individual (or pair, or small group) conferences with students outside class, usually during the teacher's office hours. Some possibilities:

- No scheduled conferences outside class. The teacher "mini-conferences" with students during class as other students work individually, with a partner, or with a small group on highly structured writing tasks and activities.
- One set of required student conferences early in the semester—one class cancelled, and conferences held in lieu of that class. The advantage: to get to know each student's writing strengths and weaknesses.
- Voluntary conferences for any students when they believe they need help. The advantage: opportunities for students for whom conferencing is genuinely helpful to more fully participate in their learning processes.
- A regular conferencing schedule for all students—one class cancelled in favor of several small-group conferences, and the conferences are held during that class time. The advantage: group conferencing can increase student-to-student feedback and learning.

NOTE: If students participate in conferences, they need specialized training that includes in-class role-play activities to prepare them for the experience.

Classroom Conferencing

Students can also participate in somewhat less formal conferencing situations. For example, the teacher can plan for a class period designated specifically to work with individual student conferences (e.g., as students work on drafts at the computers). Even less formal are the very short conferences ("mini-conferences") during class; teachers "stop by" as other students work individually, in pairs, or in small groups.

The advantages of student conferences:

- Often students are able to hear information—teacher comments, for example—better than they can read it.
- Students can immediately question what they do not understand.
- Teachers can gather information about what students do and do not know.
- Teachers can more easily individualize student remediation.

If these beliefs are part of your philosophy, for more advanced student writers you might consider one or more of the following response approaches:

1. Looking at one <u>piece</u> of each student's draft, whichever piece the student can formulate specific questions or specific directions about ("Please look at my first body paragraph. Do I have enough good evidence?"). The advantage: students must first evaluate their own writing and decide what to submit and what to ask about.
2. Offering to look at one or two drafts <u>total</u> for each student during the entire course—a draft, for example, the student has worked hard on and is still genuinely unsure about. The advantage: students assume responsibility for selecting the paper on which they want teacher feedback during their writing process. (Either students who do not want teacher feedback need not submit a paper, or all students must submit one draft.)

Defining Your Philosophy of Response[6]

Here is an opportunity to review or develop your own philosophy of response. The following process asks you to consider each step of responding in terms of (a) your expectations and (b) student success in meeting your expectations. You are asked to reflect on reasons for effective and ineffective student papers and to review your expectations on the basis of student performance. The result should give you insights into your philosophy of response.

1. Reflect on the assignment, the purpose, and the reader(s) for the assignment.
2. Carefully review the criteria you (and perhaps the students) determined would be used to evaluate the assignment. (See Chapters 15 and 16 for further discussion of Evaluation.)
3. Consider your expectations about the student responses to the assignment.
4. Read several of the student papers quickly—perhaps the entire set of student papers—without making a mark on the papers. Instead:
   a. Gather information (and take notes for yourself) about the ways students focused on the overall topic, used language, and presented their material.
   b. Look for patterns of successful and unsuccessful responses to the assignment.
5. Reconsider (and perhaps modify) your expectations.
6. Consider your individual students' preferences about teacher-response.
   a. Oral discussion through individual or group conferencing?
   b. Written notes, comments?
   c. Audiotaped responses?
7. What response elements are you most comfortable with?
   a. Written
      (1) pen, highlighter, pencil (color? size?)
      (2) underlining, checking, circling, arrows, and so on
      (3) prioritized errors in a different color? asterisked?
      (4) where?
         • cover sheet   • margins
         • end of text   • separate sheet
   b. Computer
      (1) in capital letters in text?
      (2) use of response software like
         • Microsoft Word "Notes"
         • Adobe Acrobat
         • Microsoft Word "Post-It Notes"?
   c. Audiotaped comments?

8. Review your approach to written response of organization and content:
   a. Short, clear questions in the margin?
   b. Suggestions for
      (1) exact, detailed additions?
      (2) general direction for a revision?
      (3) resources for the student to consult?[7]
   c. Consider your students' preferences for your written responses?
9. Review your approach to student grammar and structural error:
   a. Mark every error equally?
   b. If not, which will you mark?
   c. Which will you focus on for the writer?
   d. Which will you correct yourself without comment? Why?
   e. Which may you ignore? Why?
10. Consider the impact of your end comments (at the end of the student writing assignment).
    a. Focus on what? (see your criteria for evaluation)
    b. Summarize most important points of your response for the student?
    c. Positive and/or negative comments?[8]
    d. Refer students to viable sources of assistance? (a language laboratory, the campus writing center, an online writing center, an ESL handbook, peer tutors?)
    e. Consider individual student preferences for your end responses?

Endnotes

1. Ferris, D., & Hedgcock, J. (2005). *Teaching ESL composition: Purpose, process, and practice* (2nd ed.). Mahwah, NJ: Erlbaum.
2. Ashwell, T. (2000). Patterns of teacher response to student writing in a multi-draft composition classroom: Is content feedback followed by form feedback the best method? *Journal of Second Language Writing, 9,* 227–258.
3. Ferris, D. R. (2003). *Response to student writing.* Mahwah, NJ: Erlbaum.
4. Reid, J. (1994). Responding to ESL students' texts: The myths of appropriation. *TESOL Quarterly, 28,* 273–292.
5. For valuable insights on how to prepare ESL students for writing conferences, see Goldstein, L. M. & Conrad, S. M. (1990). Student input and negotiation of meaning in ESL writing conferences. *TESOL Quarterly, 24,* 443–460.

6. Ferris, D. (1999). One size does not fit all: Response and revision issues for immigrant student writers. In L. Harklau, K. M. Losey., & M. Siegal (Eds.). *Generation 1.5 meets college composition* (pp. 143–157). Mahwah, NJ: Erlbaum.

7. Chandler, J. (2003). The efficacy of various kinds of error feedback for improvement in the accuracy and fluency of L2 student writing. *Journal of Second Language Writing, 12,* 267–296.

8. Ferris, D. R. (2004). The "grammar correction" debate in L2 writing: Where are we, and where do we go from here? (and what do we do in the meantime . . . ?). *Journal of Second Language Writing, 13,* 49–62.

Responding to Student Writing

You may respond directly on a student's paper—in the margins, and/or at the end of the paper—or online, or orally in conference, or on audiotape. In each case, the overall process of responding is similar. Following are suggestions and advice based on information from experienced teachers.

Before Responding

Before you respond to students' papers, assume the persona of a student in your class and try writing the assignment yourself.

> NOTE: Writing your own assignments can be a humbling experience!

Then, as discussed in the previous chapter, read through a selection of all the students' papers quickly; see the ways students fulfill your expectations. Finally, begin the actual response process and, as you respond, think again of your written response to your assignment. Remember, too, that the papers do not exist in a void. Think about ways your students might respond to your feedback.

1. Read each student's writing again, slowly, considering each student's probable initial response to your marks and remarks.
2. Base your responses on your philosophy. In what ways will you focus your comments on:
   a. Organization (rhetoric)
   b. Content (ideas, evidence)
   c. Context (awareness of audience and purpose)
   d. Language (grammar, sentence structure, vocabulary, etc.)
3. You will no doubt develop a system to mark the language errors in whatever way seems:
   a. Most efficient
   b. Most effective for each student
4. Remember that your responses to your students' writing give you the opportunity to provide different insights as an "outside" reader that will open the door to student revising ("re-visioning": looking again at the written draft and making appropriate, logical changes).
5. Your feedback, your descriptive comments and interventions, provides students with motivation for successful revision, especially if you comment with these expectations:
   a. Revision will occur.
   b. Cognitive change/development will occur.
6. Suggestions:
   a. Point out to your students the different ways you respond (abbreviated marks, written phrases in the margins, a summary note at the end); students will be surprised that so much goes into your responses.
   b. Consider discovering how students react to your responses and how they would change your approach in some way; it's possible that some small change might result in better, more responsible student revisions.
   c. In your responses, do not ask a question if you know the answer to it; students recognize the condescension immediately.
   d. Be careful not to allow language error to contaminate the content of your students' papers; language is only one component of at least three (language, organization, and content) that make up student writing.
   e. Survey your students about which part(s) of your responses benefit them most and why. For instance, students might write a number on a scale of 1 to 5 on the cover page of each of their papers, indicating how much feedback or detail they want.

After Responding

1. Recheck your marks and remarks:
   a. Are they clear, accurate, and relevant?
   b. Will they draw the student back into the writing process to revise?

   NOTE: It's amazing how many errors (like omitted words) I catch in my responses!

2. What are your goals for the students as you return their papers with your responses?
   a. Carefully reread their papers?
   b. Look at everything you marked or wrote?
   c. Respond to everything you marked or wrote?
   d. Fix every error you marked?
   e. Decide whether to take your advice?
3. Which areas will you work on during class with all the students? Why?
4. Teacher Sharon Cavusgil offers this tip: "I teach my students how to read my comments. For example, they should start at the top and reread their paper and the comments as they come—not read my comments out of context."[1]

The Result of Teacher Response: Revision (Again!)

The logical consequence of any response process is that the student writer is pulled back into the writing process. If you have persuaded the students about the value of revision, you should have little difficulty encouraging students to look carefully at the peer or teacher response and then to make reasoned decisions about revisions that will improve their writing.

Research on composing and revising strategies in drafting, with both native English writers and second language writers of English, has shown that writers differ in their approaches to both. However, both strategies are essential to effective writing. In the same way you introduce students to different prewriting and composing skills, you might want to ask students to discuss their revision preferences and strategies.

Explanation

For some writers, revision processes occur as an integral part of the composing processes: write, revise, write, revise—with revision stimulating further momentum into writing. At the other extreme, writers compose stream-of-consciousness prose, fully expecting to select and revise major parts of their writing as they "discover" what they really want to communicate. For other writers, writing is distinct from revising; ongoing revising interrupts their writing processes. For still others (called "back-burners"—that is, they do most of their prewriting and composing internally, mentally rehearsing words, sentences, even paragraphs), revision is little more than simple editing. Their first drafts are often close to their final drafts.

Revision that follows teacher response to the student text differs from student-initiated revision. When you return student drafts that you have responded to, make sure the students know you expect them to spend at least as much time revising their writing as you spent responding to it. But understand that students may have varying degrees of competence in revising skills and strategies. Mature, experienced writers are capable of major (global, overall) revisions: reordering sentences and paragraphs, adding or eliminating substantial amounts of material, rewriting introductions or conclusions. Less experienced writers often make only discrete changes: correcting a spelling error, combining two sentences. Students who are developing writers rarely have global revision skills. Therefore, teacher support and encouragement are essential.

Teaching Suggestion

The teacher is primarily responsible for demonstrating, analyzing, and modeling revision skills and strategies as students draft their essays. I bring whatever I am working on to class, and I model revision for the class by marking transparencies of my own writing. Students are often surprised (and may be initially shocked) to see that I'm on my ninth draft and that I mark up my own writing even more severely (and certainly with less courtesy) than I do theirs. Originally, I worried that I might lose students' respect; now I realize that they appreciate knowing that experienced writers also struggle.

Similar intervention in the revising process can use student samples in various steps of the revising process: analyzing feedback, changing content, correcting errors, and so on.

Student Samples with Teacher Response

Example 1

Background: High Beginning or Low Intermediate class; early in the semester; students are learning or reviewing paragraph form and practicing the use of specific detail.

Assignment: Describe the most interesting person you know, and write why this person is so interesting.

> The most interesting person I know is my friend, Charla. She lives in an apartment near my family's apartment. She is interested because she always thinks of new things to do. When we get together after class and she will talks about the movie star she saw on TV or someone she talked to in class. Sometimes I will know about the movie, but her story is still interesting. She makes jokes about things and tells me about people. In conclusion, Charla is a good friend and a good person.

Teacher Response: The student sends her paragraph to her teacher by email, and the teacher responds by emailing his comments to the student.

Content questions: I can see from your examples that Charla is a lot of fun to talk with. So I understand when you call her a "good friend." But I don't understand why you call her a "good person." Please think about examples that you can add to help me understand better.

Grammar to correct and to add to your grammar list:

Sentence #3: "interested" is wrong. Do you remember our lesson about the difference between "interested" and "interesting"? Please check your notes and then let's talk about that change.

Sentence #4:
1. Take out either "When" or "and" (but not both!). That way, your sentence structure will be correct.
2. Remember that with words like "will," you always use the simple form of the verb. So use "talk" instead of "talks."

Vocabulary: You use the word "interesting" too much. What's a more specific word you can use to describe her stories? Perhaps you should check your dictionary.

Revision:
1. Add information to explain why Charla is a good person.
2. Use more exact adjectives than "interesting."

3. Fix the grammar.
4. Paper due Monday.

Example 2

<u>Background:</u> High Intermediate class; two-thirds of the way through the semester;

<u>Assignment:</u> Select a product that interests you. Write an essay that compares two commercial websites that advertise that product. Develop criteria to evaluate both websites, and demonstrate why one website is preferable to the other.

<u>Student Sample:</u> The first nearly complete draft of the essay. Before the teacher received this draft, here are some of the steps students in the class had completed for this assignment.

1. Students had discussed the assignment in small groups to make sure they understood it.
2. Teacher and students reviewed and discussed the use of the Internet and the process of finding two commercial websites that advertised products of comparable quality and price.
3. Teacher and students discussed two ways to present comparison/contrast information.
4. Students completed exercises to help them learn the two forms of comparison/contrast paragraph organization.
5. Individual students selected their products and reported them to the class.
6 Students met in small groups to discuss criteria for evaluation of commercial websites.
7. Individual students wrote thesis statements on the chalkboard which were discussed by the teacher and the whole class.
8. Students selected the specific criteria they would use to evaluate the websites.
9. Students wrote their background paragraphs.
10. Students met in pairs to respond to partner's background paragraph.
11. Teacher and students reviewed and discussed APA citation format for Internet sources.
12. Students completed their end-of-text reference lists in class while the teacher mini-conferenced with individual students.
13. Students wrote their first complete drafts.

14. In class, students reviewed and edited their own first drafts, using an author-response form.
15. Students met in pairs and responded to their partners' first drafts, using a peer response form; students revised and rewrote their drafts.
16. Students turned in their drafts for teacher-response.

Choosing a Good Website

Muang Saechao

Tired of shopping on the net and ~~can~~ not figure out^(ing) which website to choose from? Shopping on the net is good way to shop because you won't have to get out of the house, drive, get stuck in traffic, and stay in a department store for hours. Well, I'm tired of not know^(ing) which is the best ~~way~~ website to shop ~~with~~^(VT), so I develop some criteria to help make shopping on the net easier. I browsed the Internet and found two ^(Good) clothing websites; American Eagle and Old Navy. They both advertise ^(Thesis) and sell the same stuff, but ~~the~~ Old Navy's site have^(agr) more graphics, is more informative and has good links. I chose these two websites because since the winter season is coming soon, I am looking for jackets to keep me warm throughout the season. ^(agr)

While browsing these two websites, ~~yhr msin~~ the criteria I used was graphics, information and links to evaluate these two websites. According to the Longman Dictionary of American English, graphics were defined as, "the activity of drawing pictures or designs, or the designs or picture themsleves" (Longman, 2002), p. 343). Graphics are an important ~~thing to look at~~ because they are the first thing people ^(Good use) notice. Information is the facts or details that tell you something ^(of a) about a situation , person, event, etc. (Longman, 2002) (p. 407) ^(quotation) Information is also important because if the site doesn't have ^(& in text) information, for example on size, how would you know what sizes they ^(citation!) have. Links are also important, they are short for hyperlinks; Hyperlinks are defined as a special picture or word on a computer screen that you click^(ed) in order to move quickly to a place where you can find more information (Longman, 2002, p. 390).

The first thing I looked at was the graphics. I want something that will get my attention. To get my attention, it has to have pictures and be colorful. For example, if there is a jacket on sale, it has to be colorful ~~to get my attention~~ so it will be the first thing I see. The American Eagle webpage does not have good graphics. It doesn't have many pictures. It only has a picture of a jacket and not many colors. X I'm not very interested in this site because it don't stand out like the Old Navy's site. The Old Navy site has excellent graphics. The color is bright, and the page showed a picture of a family, a mother, father and a baby. They have the jackets on sale and made the page bright so I will look at their jackets. The other thing is the text. It was large and easy to read. After looking at the picture I just skim the caption and it would tell me what kind of jacket it is and if it is on sale or not.

Please take out all words that contain "thing" and replace them with more specific words.

Another thing I looked at was how much is given on the site. Old Navy's webpage has very good information. It has information on how to apply for an Old Navy credit card, where to find a store by you sign up for email, and get updates on the latest styles, details, offers and events. It has information on customer service and the site and many links. If you are looking for women' clothing, you click on women and from there it shows the clothes. Inside that page, there are also links. These links are categorized by what the item is. For example, you are in the woman pages and from there is a list from shirts to pants, shoes to accessories, and to clearance items.

Old Navy would probably be the easier one for most people to use and especially those who aren't familiar with computers because it gives out more information. American Eagle is not really an attention grabber and is really dull on color. It only has one color, the navy blue. Old navy has more graphics, so it probably attracts more people to explore the site rather than just glancing at what is on sale. I would choose Old Navy to shop with because it has more pictures that attract me to the site. It also has more information for me to read through, and more links for me to view. Besides all that, the Old Navy site has more causal clothes and is targeted to all people, having

clothes for men, babies, and even maternity clothes for pregnant
mothers. ~~On the other hand~~, By browsing the Old Navy website, I can
shop for myself and do Christmas shopping for my family members.

References

American Eagle Outfitters Homepage. (2003). Retrieved October 16,
2004: http://www.ae.com

Longman. (2002) *Dictionary of American English* (2nd ed.).New York : Longman

Old Navy Homepage. (2003). Welcome to Old Navy. Retrieved October 16,
2004: http://www.oldnavy.com/asp.home.html?wdid=0.

Teacher Response:

Muang: This is a very promising draft. The thesis statement lists the
essay's main ideas clearly. Your body paragraphs have many good details,
and with some development they will become more effective. However,
your topic sentences need to be revised first, so you will have well-defined,
controlling ideas to shape the body paragraphs—including the details in
those paragraphs.

Go back to your essay map to make sure your essay follows it more
accurately. Also, revise your conclusion to make sure it reflects what you
actually say in the essay. My comments in the margins should help. Good
luck! GN[2]

Endnotes

1. Sharon Cavusgil generously agreed to read and edit this manuscript. She
   deserves a medal as well as my gratitude.
2. Courtesy of Gabriella Nuttall, author of *College Writing 3*.

Chapter **15**

Final Drafts: Getting Ready to Evaluate/Assess Student Writing

On the day students turn in the final drafts of their paragraphs or essays, consider spending that class day (when the students are often tired and unwilling to do much more than get rid of their papers) having students work with their finished papers.

1. Ask students to complete one of more of the following (or other questions that relate directly to what you are currently teaching).
    a. Underline the thesis and the topic sentences
    b. Label the introduction and conclusion techniques (in the margin)
    c. Label the techniques of support used in three body paragraphs (in the margin)
    d. Label the methods of development used in three body paragraphs (in the margin)
    e. At the end of the essay, write:
        • The total number of words in the essay
        • The intended reader(s)
        • The purpose of the essay

2. Also ask students to read three essays (not including their own) and to take brief notes about each (e.g., writer, title, important ideas).
   a. At the end of that process, each student must be able to state, "I liked X's paper about Y because . . . . Their answers should be directly related to the rhetoric or the content of the paper; general or vague words (e.g., *interesting*) are unacceptable.
   b. As students give their reasons, write those reasons on the board. Possibilities include:
      ". . . the first sentence made me want to read more."
      ". . . I learned about the topic by reading details like XXX."
      ". . . the body paragraphs were easy to follow."
   c. At the end, ask the student writers to observe the list carefully: "Here's what your readers thought were especially good."

   NOTE: Initially, the comments will not be as insightful as they will be later in the semester. But any student whose essay is targeted for praise will feel wonderful—a response from a real reader, a member of the classroom writing community!

Postmortems

Students learn as they think about their writing, but they rarely spend time analyzing their papers. After they have written their papers, they regard the task as completely finished, "dead" as a proverbial doornail. I ask students to complete a "postmortem," a metacognitive exercise in which students have to remember their writing processes and report on them.

1. Write five categories at the top of the board: Easy, Difficult, Problems, Solutions, and Learned. Draw vertical lines between the categories.
2. Ask the students to take turns writing a short phrase in each of the columns and to put their initials after each; if another student has already written that phrase, students can put a check mark beside it.
3. Discuss the information from the postmortem. Have students notice that during the course:
   a. Some items that are difficult for one student are "easy" for another
   b. Some items that are initially "difficult" for most students move to the "easy" list

   NOTE: You might ask the first five students who finish to make a list of each column so that you have a record.

For later papers, students can write a postmortem at the end of their final drafts. Doing so avoids the problem of students who simply wait for others to do the work on the board and then put check marks next to them.

Here is a sample postmortem (limited for the sake of space—usually every student in the class writes in every column).

Sample

Background: Adv. ESL Class, third week of the semester
Assignment: Respond to a survey about learning styles, and support your agreement and/or disagreement with the results with examples from your previous experience

Postmortem Exercise on Writing Process				
Easy	Difficult	Problem(s) →	Solution(s)	Learned
agreeing and disagreeing	actually writing!	being → clear	go to Writing Lab	how to analyze data
making a table	organization	background → paragraph	read packet again	how to make a table
organization	limiting my information	organization →	use just two examples, not four	how to give personal examples
my experiences	starting	procrastination →	focus on task	how to gather information
	keeping it short			

Why Evaluate Student Writing?

Simply put, assessment is part of the teacher's job. Here are some reasons for assessment of student writing:

- Determining placement
- Diagnosing students' strengths and weaknesses
- Identifying achievement or progress
- Ranking students with other students (a) in the class or (b) in the program
- Providing information about students' readiness to pass to the next level of writing

In addition, evaluating student writing from class assignments (in-class and outside class) demonstrates for the teacher:

- How well the assignment worked
- What students are learning or not learning
- Whether students are meeting course objectives

It also allows teachers to provide students with feedback concerning their strengths and weaknesses and to offer advice or feedback to help students improve their writing.

Students are aware of the frequency of evaluation in our lives: "Great weather!" "Awful movie!" They also understand the need for evaluation of their writing as part of the course and their final grade. In fact, assessment is an integral part of formal learning, and it begins the first day of class.

1. Your policy sheet or syllabus (Chapter 6) has clearly delineated the basis and processes for course grades.
2. You will have begun assessing their written work during the first days of class. You at least have marked—responded to—and possibly "graded" their diagnostic writing sample(s). (See Chapter 8.)
3. You also will no doubt be assessing student work in these ways:
   a. Indirectly (e.g., by observing their work in class)
   b. Directly—grading periodic quizzes, participation in group work, in-class writing activities, and the like

Just as important, you have probably already begun to ask students to evaluate:

1. Their "warm-ups" (e.g., "What was the best part of the last class? Why?") (See Chapter 7, "Metacognitive Writing.")
   a. Class activities (e.g., "Did this activity help you understand X? Why or why not?")
   b. Course material (e.g., "Which writing assignment from this course will help you most with future college writing? Explain your choice.")
2. Their own writing
3. Their progress in the class

Despite the myths that students sometimes hold, teacher assessment of EAP ESL student writing, like responding (in the previous chapters), is neither a random nor an arbitrary activity. It requires teachers to develop a philosophy of evaluation and to communicate that philosophy to ESL writers in their classes. For students, **evaluation should never be mysterious**; students should never think, even in jest, that instructors don't really read their papers, that they "just toss the papers down a flight of stairs, and the ones on the first step get As."

Rather, it is the teacher's responsibility to persuade their students that:

- Teachers use their prior knowledge and expertise to develop specific criteria
- These criteria are based on a complex set of variables that can be explained
- Each instructor has her or his assessment "standards" that the instructor must explain to the students, clearly and completely[1]

Developing Criteria for Assessment

The first step in fair evaluation of student writing is developing criteria. The second step is making those criteria available to the student writers. To achieve fairness and to ensure that students will learn from your evaluation, develop clear assessment criteria for each writing assignment. Then, most important, share those criteria with the students. A written set of assessment criteria designed and handed out with the written directions of the writing assignment is the first step in unambiguous, comprehensible evaluation. (See the following "cover sheet.") Going through those criteria with the students ensures that they have confronted the criteria. You may even have students help create the criteria for some writing assignments.

NOTE: Of course, you will have to follow the criteria closely as you assess students' papers in order to maintain fairness.

Below are two sets of criteria that can be adapted for a variety of writing tasks.

Set 1

Evaluation Cover Sheet: Advanced Writing Class[2]

Assignment-Based Criteria
Fulfills the goals stated for the assignment   _____
Looks like the assigned writing
   (summary? research? report?)   _____

Content-Based Criteria
Is substantive   _____
Shows understanding of key concepts   _____
Includes original insights and synthesis   _____

Presentation/Organization-Based Criteria
Paper follows through on what the introduction sets out   _____
Paper is sequenced in a clearly discernible way   _____
Parts of the paper are well connected to each
   (coherence)   _____
Source materials are cited appropriately and
   integrated with the text   _____

Language-Based Criteria
Grammar and usage   _____
Sentence structure and variety   _____
Vocabulary   _____

Set 2

Evaluation Cover Sheet: High Intermediate Writing Class

Essay Title: _____

	Strengths	Problem Area
Purpose and audience		
Focus		
Development		
Organization		
Grammar/Sentence Structure		
Suggestions for revision:		
Writer's plans for revision:		

Set 3

Evaluation Cover Sheet: Advanced Writing Class

Problem-Solving Paper: Evaluation Criteria

	Points Earned	Comments
Problem: Show that a problem exists and needs attention (introduction, background paragraph)	20	
Solution: Persuasive presentation of solutions (compare/contrast body paragraphs, feasibility paragraph)	30	
Implementation: (Call for Action) timeline paragraph concluding paragraph	10	
Persuasive rejection of objections (refutation paragraph)	10	
Overall effectiveness		
audience awareness	5	
overall organization	10	
coherence	5	
language	10	
TOTAL	100	Final Score: _____

Cover Sheets and Evaluation

A cover sheet with the writing assignment on the front (and space for the student's name, course, and other expected information) and an assessment sheet on the back is one way to ensure that students:

- Keep and therefore have access to the actual assignment
- Read and understand the criteria by which their papers will be evaluated

  NOTE: Making students aware of your evaluation criteria also answers the question that sometimes arises: "I turned this very paper in to my instructor in X, and I got an A, so why did I get a C on it from you?"

  Most assessment cover sheets (like the three previous sets of criteria) contain the criteria by which the assignment will be evaluated, as well as spaces for comments and questions. Here are two cover sheets with the spaces for comments removed. Again, I have provided minimum background information to contextualize the examples.

Cover Sheet 1

Background: High Intermediate EAP students preparing for college work
Timeline: Midsemester of a sixteen-week semester

Name: _____ Date: _____

Explaining Essay

- Directions followed, including Special Instructions: _____
- Clear thesis statement and topic sentences: _____
- Appropriate background paragraph detail: _____
- Clear and interesting supporting material: _____
- Introductory and Concluding techniques: _____
Grade:
organization: _____ content: _____ language: _____

Comments: _____

Cover Sheet 2

<u>Background</u>: Advanced writing class, EAP students preparing for college work

<u>Timeline</u>: Week twelve of a sixteen-week semester; assignment: summarize and analyze a reading

---

Name: _____ Date: _____

Summary-Analysis Essay

- Directions followed, including Postmortem Memo: _____
- Background paragraph (summary): _____
- Clear overall and inner paragraph organization of body paragraphs:

  _____

- Original, adequate supporting materials/evidence:

  _____

- Appropriate and adequate use of coherence techniques:

  _____

Grade:

organization: _____ content: _____ language: _____

Comments: _____

As difficult as assessment is, it is at the heart of an EAP writing class. Students will be inordinately interested; almost all will look at their grades first when papers are returned.

> NOTE: Unless you require (and grade) careful revision and/or require a modified portfolio course, students may never even look at the returned paper again.

Assumptions about Evaluation

The following information probably does no more than remind you of the bases for the evaluation of writing. However, you may want to discuss some or all of these assumptions with your students, who rarely think about such things.

1. The goals of evaluation are (a) long-term improvement and (b) recognition of progress.
2. Planning and evaluating are complementary and continuous processes in assessment.
3. Teachers evaluate what they teach, and students are aware of those criteria.
4. Correction of error is effective when the feedback concerning the error is clear:
   a. Students can immediately identify the error as an error (and why).
   b. Students can remediate the error and learn from their revision.
5. Feedback (response and evaluation) will be less effective, and possibly ineffective, without follow-up such as the following:

   Participatory class discussion   Group correction and practice
   Metacognitive journal entries   Required (possible graded) revisions

   (See Chapter 7)   (See Chapter 5)
6. Teacher comments about language and content can be given at the same time without overburdening the students.
7. Students' papers should reflect ongoing learning experiences, skills, and strategies as the course progresses and should be evaluated on both prior and (especially) current learning (an indication of overall proficiency, as well as current progress).
8. Teacher evaluation (assigning grades) is expected by the students and so is probably easier for them to receive than for many teachers to assign.
9. Assigning multiple grades (e.g., for organization, content, and language) for major papers is one way of:
   a. Giving students insight into their strengths and weaknesses
   b. Assigning a very low grade (even an F) in one area without guilt

Explanation

I give three grades for each major essay. Each "counts" equally, so the students know (a) their overall (average) grade and (b) their writing strengths and weaknesses.

Example:

1. **Organization:** use of writing conventions to achieve overall, inner paragraph expectations of the academic reader; includes use of thesis statement and topic sentences, introductory and concluding forms and functions
2. **Content:** clear communication of ideas, opinions, and support that fulfill the assignment; includes quality and quantity of information, appropriate and adequate use of supporting examples, experience, and detail, and level of persuasiveness
3. **Language:** includes grammar, mechanics (e.g., spelling, punctuation, capitalization), sentence structure, choice of appropriate vocabulary and formality, and overall impact of fluency and accuracy on readers

So, a grade of A/C/F describes a paper with high-quality organization, average content, and serious language problems. The overall single grade is an average—in this case, C.

Endnotes

1. Ferris, D. L., & Hedgcock, I. (2005). *Teaching ESL composition* (2nd ed.). Mahwah, NJ: Erlbaum.
2. Sharon Cavusgil (Georgia State University) suggests that the percentage of each paper that is used to calculate each student's final grade should increase as the term progresses. For example, the first paper might be worth 10 percent, the second and third 15 percent, and the fourth paper 20 percent.

Chapter 16

Evaluating Student Writing

Despite an enormous number of articles about evaluating writing, no "standard" set of criteria has been developed to evaluate student writing, probably because (at least):

- Writing results from an extremely complex set and series of human skills and strategies; evaluating each, and each in its relation to others, would be an overwhelming task.
- There are many different kinds of writing, and even of academic writing (genres), each of which may require a more or less different set of grading criteria.
- Different external purposes for writing (e.g., placement, progress) demand different criteria.
- Teachers base their approach to evaluation on their individual backgrounds: reading, philosophies of teaching writing, the colleagues they admire, and prior experiences.

As a consequence, for teachers, the responsibility of forming a philosophy of assessment begins well before the final student drafts are turned in.

1. The writing assignment is carefully developed with course curriculum and program goals in mind. (See Chapter 1.)
   a. Because writing assignments are a form of testing, they define the emphases and the structure of the writing course.

    b. The needs of students in the class are an integral part of the assignment.

    c. The purpose of each assignment also reflects some of the instructor's values.

2. The assignment is clearly defined and precisely articulated for the students. Students learn:

    a. The reasons for the assignment

        1.) within the course and curriculum

        2.) as preparation for future academic writing

    b. The expectations of the teacher developer/assigner/evaluator

3. The students are given opportunities, including adequate time, to identify, learn, and practice the strategies and skills essential to completing the assignment successfully.

Other concerns in forming a philosophy of assessment include:

1. Whether all written work will be turned in for grading

    a. Early drafts reviewed by peers but not responded to by the teacher?

    b. Later draft I reviewed and responded to by the teacher?

    c. Only the final draft responded to and graded by the teacher?

    d. Only three out of every ten journal entries or metacognitive entries graded by the teacher?

2. Whether written work will be graded in a variety of ways

    a. Quizzes graded in class by peers; the teacher records the grades?

    b. In-class writing graded holistically without teacher response? And no revision?

    c. Smaller writing assignments graded with +, ✓, or –.

3. Whether students will be involved in designing/selecting criteria for (some?) writing assignments

This chapter focuses on the processes that result in the development of a philosophy of writing assessment.

Assessment and Language Error

Error is at the basis of all discussions of ESL EAP writing assessment. We can define "language accuracy" as the student's facility in using the grammatical system of standard edited English in such categories as sentence structure, word form, word order, and verb tenses.

Explanation

Historically, the opposite of "language accuracy" was called "language fluency." That is, students write without much hesitation, but their language is flawed with structural errors. Today, this false opposition has been discarded: both international and U.S. resident/immigrant students can have both written accuracy and fluency, or neither, as well as having one without the other.

Although ESL teachers once thought of language error as deviant behavior (the result of laziness and stupidity), error is now seen as a natural phenomenon in learning of all kinds: learning to ski or play tennis, to word-process or analyze literature, to make jewelry or write academic papers. Of course, errors in writing can be the result of haste, inattention, memory lapse, or even laziness, and for ESL writers, timed writing situations can easily result in "performance errors."

But in general, **ESL writing errors are not random, sporadic, or deviant. Instead, they are often systematic, regular, and rule-governed— the result of intelligence, not stupidity.** Research has demonstrated that ESL written errors are the result of conscious or unconscious attempts by students to use what they have learned. The English language, with such errors, has even been given a name: an *interlanguage.* According to research, a student's interlanguage is dynamic; that is, it is in a constant state of change as the student learns more about the language and begins to assemble rules that are correct.[1]

Explanation

For international students, research has even identified three major factors that are responsible for many (conscious or unconscious) ESL language errors:

1. L1 transfer: Students infer and apply ("transfer") language rules from their first (also called "original" or "heritage") language.
2. Overgeneralization: Like many L1 learners, ESL students may extend a rule past the boundaries of that rule. Young L1 children may, for instance, use such words as "eated" and "drived." L2 students may use the -*s* at the end of third-person singular verbs ("he eats") to second-person singular verbs ("you eats"). In both cases, the application of the rule is incorrect, but it is a systematic use of the rule.

3. Difficulty level: A complex language rule may be too difficult, so ESL students may make errors when they attempt to construct the form.

For U.S. resident/immigrant students, little empirical research that analyzes and categorizes error exists. But we might hypothesize that:

1. Their errors are also the result of application of conscious or unconscious rules based on language they heard as they were immersed in English.
2. If these students are still learning the language, they may be using a dynamic "interlanguage."
3. If these students are literate in their L1, they may be transferring rules from their L1, creating errors in English.
4. Almost certainly the students are overgeneralizing some of their interlanguage rules, creating rule-governed, systematic (incorrect) structures in English.
5. Some language rules may be too complex for some of these students at their current level of language knowledge; the result may be structural error.

If these hypotheses are true, then we must approach U.S. resident/immigrant students' language errors with attitudes similar to our approaches to international students' errors. To summarize the previous discussion and analysis of U.S. resident errors (in the Introduction and in Chapters 4 and 5):

- Written errors by U.S. resident students must be seen by their instructors in the context of communicative purpose.
- Student writing errors need to be prioritized if the writers are to benefit from remediation.
- Some errors are almost never 100 percent remediable. Fortunately, these errors do not usually interfere with reader comprehension. Unfortunately, they are immediately visible and at least irritating to academic readers.
- For such errors (in particular, articles and prepositions), U.S. resident writers should spend their time more wisely on content and organization of their ideas and on other, more serious errors. Then they should ask a native speaker of English for assistance in identifying and correcting the articles and prepositions in their writing.

Assessment and Rhetorical Error

In addition to language problems, EAP ESL writing students can demonstrate limited knowledge of the conventions (the rhetoric) of academic writing. Many factors can be evaluated: content, purpose, audience, writing conventions (reader expectations for organization, cohesion, and unity).

Teacher-researcher Barbara Kroll divides ESL writing students into two broad categories: plus (or minus) syntax and plus (or minus) rhetoric.[2] She defines rhetorical competence as writing that:

1. Limits and focuses on the topic in a manner appropriate to its overall approach and length
2. Remains focused on the topic throughout
3. Creates and uses paragraphs effectively
4. Maintains a consistent point of view
5. Sequences ideas in a logical manner
6. Uses coherence and cohesion devices appropriately and as necessary

Explanation

Kroll's simplified analysis of basic differences between international and resident student writing is still insightful. International student writing may demonstrate grammatical understanding (especially at the most advanced levels of language proficiency), but these students' relatively limited knowledge of U.S. academic writing conventions results in categorizing their written work as

$$+\text{syntax} \quad \text{but} \quad -\text{ rhetoric.}$$

In contrast, resident students, particularly those who have had experiences in U.S. classrooms, may write in acceptable academic rhetorical conventions (e.g., the "hamburger paragraph"), but their language is flawed:

$$-\text{ language} \quad \text{but} \quad +\text{ rhetoric.}$$

(Of course, some students, both international and resident, may be + language and + rhetoric while others may be − language and − rhetoric.)

Such analysis has consequences for curriculum development, lesson plans, and presentation of materials, particularly in classes with both international and U.S. resident/immigrant student writers.

NOTE: Responding and evaluating ESL EAP student writing includes attention to both language and rhetorical issues.

Grading Scales

Generally, grading scales for ESL writing are defined in two categories: analytic and holistic. Each has different purposes.

NOTE: The first two sets of "general" criteria given previously concentrate on a more "holistic" approach. The third is more "analytic."

Analytic scoring identifies and evaluates various individual components of a piece of writing. Each component is assigned a numerical value (or, sometimes, a letter grade). Often, an analytic scoring guide is useful to identify the development (progress) of student writing skills. Examples that have proved useful for teachers of ESL EAP writing:

Sample Analytic Scales

1. Low Intermediate Writing Class
   Start with 100 points and subtract points for each error or deficiency:

incorrect verb tense(s)	10 points
word form error(s)	10 points
lack of vocabulary accuracy (wrong word)	10 points, etc.
Total:	X points

   Grade: X%

2. Intermediate Writing Class
   Give a percentage of the overall grade for each writing component:

introduction	10%
topic sentences	20%
sentence structure	20%, etc.
Total:	X%
Grade: X%	

3. High Intermediate Writing Class
   Rate each feature for its overall merit by circling a number.

   Introduction
       Informative title and lead-in   1 2 3 4 5
       Clear thesis statement   1 2 3 4 5
           Total _____ (out of 10)

   Support
       Specific examples and details   4 8 12 16 20
       Connections between ideas   4 8 12 16 20
           Total _____ (out of 40)

   Organization
       Transitions   2 4 6 8 10
       Paragraph unity and coherence   2 4 6 8 10, etc.
           Total _____ (out of 20)

   Grades: A = 90–100, B = 80–90, etc.

Analytic Scoring Guides for Large-Scale Evaluation

Wide-ranging, complex scoring guides like the ESL Composition Profile (below) can be used by teachers in an ESL EAP writing course, but they are more likely to be used in large-scale grading situations. For example, your writing program may have "group grading" for a common final examination given to all students in each level. That is, teachers gather together after the common finals are given and grade essays from all the classes at the level; the papers are randomized so that teachers do not grade their own students' papers. Usually, such grading sessions are based on a large-scale rubric like the following. An important part of the scoring process is "standardizing the teachers"—that is, teachers read and score selected "benchmark" papers according to the scoring guide until they score papers similarly.

Teachers read each paper and assign (a) analytic scores, as in the ESL Composition Profile below or (b) a single holistic score, as in the Test of Written English Guide. In both cases, each paper is read twice, with the first score hidden from the second reader. If the scores of the two readers differ substantially, an authoritative grader (e.g., the writing curriculum supervisor, the course coordinator) gives the paper a third, careful reading and assigns a score or grade. Notice:

1. The overall number of points changes with each category, an indication of which categories the profile writers considered more or less important.
2. The "cutoff" scores (pass to the next level or fail; ready or not ready for academic work; classified as "advanced," "intermediate," etc.) are made by the program administrators.

If your program does not have common grading of finals, another way you might use the Composition Profile is to select criteria from the profile for use in a rubric for a student assignment. You might also use the explicit descriptive vocabulary for discussing such criteria with your students.

ESL COMPOSITION PROFILE[3]

Student _____ Date _____ Topic _____

	Score	Level	Criteria	Comments
C	30–27	EXCELLENT TO VERY GOOD: knowledgeable • substantive • thorough development of thesis • relevant to assigned topic		
O				
N	26–22	GOOD TO AVERAGE: some knowledge of subject • adequate range • limited development of thesis • mostly relevant to topic, but lacks detail		
T				
E	21–17	FAIR TO POOR: limited knowledge of subject • little substance • inadequate development of topic		
N				
T	16–13	VERY POOR: does not show knowledge of subject • non-substantive • not pertinent • OR not enough to evaluate		
O	20–18	EXCELLENT TO VERY GOOD: fluent expression • ideas clearly stated/supported • succinct • well-organized • logical sequencing • cohesive		
R				
G				
A	17–14	GOOD TO AVERAGE: somewhat choppy • loosely organized but main ideas stand out • limited support • logical but incomplete sequencing		
N				
I				
Z	13–10	FAIR TO POOR: non-fluent • ideas confused or disconnected • lacks logical sequencing and development		
A				
T				
I	9–7	VERY POOR: does not communicate • no organization • OR not enough to evaluate		
O				
N				

	Score	Level	Criteria	Comments
V O C A B U L A R Y	20–18	EXCELLENT TO VERY GOOD: sophisticated range • effective word/idiom choice and usage • word form mastery • appropriate register		
	17–14	GOOD TO AVERAGE: adequate range • occasional errors of word/idiom form, choice, usage, but *meaning not obscured*		
	13–10	FAIR TO POOR: limited range • frequent errors of word/idiom form, choice, usage • *meaning confused or obscured*		
	9–7	VERY POOR: essentially translation • little knowledge of English vocabulary, idioms, word form • OR not enough to evaluate		
L A N G U A G E U S E	25–22	EXCELLENT TO VERY GOOD: effective complex constructions • few errors of agreement, tense, number, word order/function, articles, pronouns, prepositions		
	21–18	GOOD TO AVERAGE: effective but simple constructions • minor problems in complex constructions • several errors of agreement, tense, number, word order/ function, articles, pronouns, prepositions, but *meaning seldom obscured*		
	17–11	FAIR TO POOR: major problems in simple/complex constructions • frequent errors of negation, agreement, tense, number, word order/function, articles, pronouns, prepositions and/or fragments, run-ons, deletions • *meaning confused or obscured*		
	10–5	VERY POOR: virtually no mastery of sentence construction rules • dominated by errors • does not communicate • OR not enough to evaluate		

	Score	Level	Criteria	Comments
M	5		EXCELLENT TO VERY GOOD: demonstrates mastery of conventions • few errors of spelling, punctuation, capitalization, paragraphing	
E				
C				
H	4		GOOD TO AVERAGE: occasional errors of spelling, punctuation, capitalization, paragraphing, but *meaning not obscured*	
A				
N				
I	3		FAIR TO POOR: frequent errors of spelling, punctuation, capitalization, paragraphing • poor handwriting • *meaning confused or obscured*	
C				
S				
	2		VERY POOR: no mastery of conventions • dominated by errors of spelling, punctuation, capitalization, paragraphing • handwriting illegible • OR not enough to evaluate	

TOTAL SCORE _____   READER _____   COMMENTS _____

Endnotes

1. Gass, S. M., & Selinker, L. (2001). *Second language acquisition: An introductory course* (2nd ed.). Mahwah, NJ: Erlbaum.
2. Kroll, B. (1990). The rhetoric-syntax split: Designing a curriculum for ESL students. *Journal of Basic Writing, 9*(1), 40–55.
3. Hartfiel, V. F., Hughey, J. B., Wormuth, D. R., & Jacobs, H. (1981). Composition profile. In *Testing ESL composition.* Rowley, MA: Newbury House.

Chapter **17**

Returning Evaluated Papers

The day you return student papers is never an entirely pleasant class. Suggestions:

1. Have the following policies, and communicate these policies to the students before that day. Then remind the students of these policies.
   a. Do not return papers until the end of class.
   b. Students must not speak to you that instant about their papers. They must first:
      (1) Look carefully at their papers, not just the grade(s)
      (2) Beat their pillows, call their mothers, eat chocolate . . .
      (3) Make an appointment to meet with you outside class
2. Plan a full class of activities for that day, with pair and group work included.
3. Leave fifteen minutes at the end of class to discuss the overall strengths and weaknesses of the papers (and I often apologize for my handwriting, encouraging students to ask me if they cannot read my comments).

4. (Optional) Have students write for two minutes about what comments/responses they expect on the returned papers. For example, you might ask them to write about:
    a. What they remember as the strengths and the weaknesses of this paper
    b. What they believe they might have done more effectively (and how)
    c. How successful they think this paper is in relation to previous papers (and why)

    NOTE: Do not ask them to guess their grades.

5. Remind students of your commitment to helping them improve their writing by responding to and carefully evaluating their writing.
6. Compliment student successes on the paper, and mention the most effective papers and authors by title and name.
7. Summarize and write (on the board, a transparency, or a handout) the areas of error (both content and language) that students will need to focus on as they revise.
8. Review revision processes. Write revision due dates on the board.
9. (Optional) Put a summary of the grades on the board.

Evaluation and Revision

As with teacher response, the immediate consequence of teacher evaluation should be student revision.

Teaching Suggestion

You might introduce the revision process by asking students to discuss, with partners or in small groups, the processes they go through when they first receive a graded paper. They should then list (honestly!) those steps. Almost certainly the students will list "finding the grade" as their first step, and almost certainly "thinking about how to revise the writing" will not appear on their initial list. In fact, only if you require revisions will you be able to persuade the students that such thoughts are reasonable, a next step in improving their writing.

Language Error and Revision

After you return student writing and discuss revision, your students may be interested in and capable of correcting their grammar and syntax errors. They may also be overwhelmed by your marks on their papers, however, and may not know how to revise those errors. In fact, they may not even know why some of the words have been marked as errors.[1]

> NOTE: See Chapter 18 for a discussion of teaching grammar in the writing classroom.

Using an Error Chart

Developing an error chart for student use will allow students to see their progress through a semester of writing.[2] During a full-class discussion, introduce students to error analysis. Use one or more of the student samples shown at the Houghton Mifflin website on an overhead transparency or a PowerPoint presentation, or use errors from current student papers (or from previous students' papers).

For each error, make sure students can (a) identify (recognize) exactly what the error is and (b) why it is an error. First ask if students can identify the errors. (If students cannot identify errors, they certainly cannot correct them.) If students cannot identify an error, demonstrate the problem and the solution on the chalkboard or the overhead transparency.

Next, with a transparency or PowerPoint page of the following Error Chart (and handouts for each student), ask students to record their errors on the error chart (sample error chart follows).

> NOTE: Instead of an error chart, you may decide to have students keep file cards for each writing assignment's errors or to keep a section of their writing notebook to categorize and correct their errors.

> You and the students may decide what to list:

- Just the major errors (e.g., verb tenses and forms, word choice, agreement, word order, sentence boundaries)
- Just the errors you have prioritized that the students should concentrate on correcting
- Just the errors/structures you have been teaching
- All the marked and corrected errors

Sample Error Chart

NAME _____   Class _____

ESSAY _____   Date _____

Error Type	ERROR	CORRECTION
F (word form)		
Sp (spelling)		
Ref (referent)		
Agr (subject-verb)		
WW (wrong word)		
VT (verb tense)		
R-O (run-on)		
Frag. (fragment)		

NOTE: The categories on this error chart may be modified or changed for each student essay, or they may remain the same throughout the course.

For students who do not find this process effective, the teacher might hold small-group conferences the students themselves organize—either during class or outside class. In these conferences, the students ask questions about errors they did not understand or had trouble correcting.[3]

One note of caution: Teachers and students must expect that improvement in ESL grammar and syntax will be neither quick nor easy.[4] Writing in a second language is an even more complex set of cognitive tasks than writing as a native speaker. The grammar "rules" of second language writers that have been habituated must be unlearned, and reader expectations (cultural, rhetorical, contextual, and linguistic) must be identified and fulfilled. Time, effort, understanding, energy, patience, and trust are important. Without these qualities, both teachers and ESL student writers will be frustrated.

Endnotes

1. Ferris (2003).

2. Roberts, B. J. (1991). *Can error logs raise more than consciousness? The effect of error logs on grammar feedback on ESL students' final drafts.* Unpublished master's thesis, California State University, Sacramento.

3. Goldstein, L. M., & Conrad, S. M. (1990). Student input and negotiation of meaning in ESL writing conferences. *TESOL Quarterly, 24,* 443–460.

4. Sternglass, M. S. (1997). *Time to know them: A longitudinal study of writing and learning at the college level.* Mahwah, NJ: Erlbaum.

Part **5**

Exposing Myths about Teaching Grammar

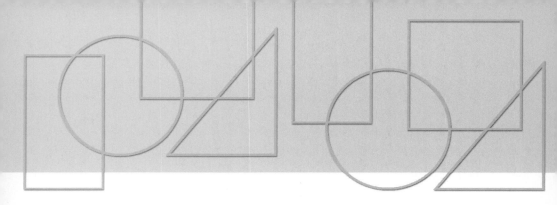

Chapter 18

Teaching Grammar in the Composition Classroom

It is intentional that the issue of grammar teaching in writing classes concludes this instructors' guide.

The purpose of an EAP ESL writing class is to prepare students for the communicative writing tasks they will encounter in college classes, from note-taking to writing research papers. Included in this purpose is writing that is rhetorically expected by the academic reader—writing that is not only fluent but also accurate.

Notice that grammar is not at the heart of a writing course. Instead, it is just part of one of the purposes. And although there are appropriate and even successful ways to teach L2 writing students about new academic structures they will practice in their writing, the organized, time-consuming teaching of grammatical structures to remediate incorrect grammar "rules"

1. is not worth substantial class time and
2. has not been shown to transfer to student writing.

I begin this chapter by exposing myths about teaching grammar (in particular, to EAP ESL resident writers). Then I give a brief rationale for selecting, diagnosing, and perhaps teaching some grammar structures in an EAP ESL writing class and finish by offering strategies for students to self-identify and prioritize their grammar study.

Should Grammar Be Part of an ESL EAP Writing Class?

The short answer to the question posed in the above heading: it depends on the students and the selection of the grammar structures. More specifically, it depends on:

1. The language proficiency of the students
2. The previous educational background of the students
3. *Who* the students are: their learning styles and strategies[1]
4. The selection of grammatical structures
   a. *What* structure is selected
   b. *How* the structure is selected
   c. *When* the structure is selected and taught
   d. *Why* the structure is selected and taught
   e. *Where* the structure is taught
   f. *How* the structure is taught[2]

What follows in this chapter may seem intimidating: a way to select and prioritize grammatical structures to teach in ESL EAP writing classes that does not follow the sequence of most grammar textbooks. Further, the research that underlies this change is relatively new, and so writing textbooks that incorporate grammar structures in this way are limited (but see the treatment of grammar in the EAS student books associated with this textbook series.).

Of course, in addition to the "Power Grammar" structures discussed below, you can certainly identify individual students' problems with grammar, sentence structure, and mechanics and advise or require students to use a handbook, an online grammar website, or the resource pages of an OWL to try to remediate serious individual problems.

In other words, do not despair. At the least, this chapter should encourage you to spend class time teaching specifically identified contextualized grammar structures that have a high probability of improving students' written syntax. For example, following are structures that research has shown every ESL EAP writer should learn and practice.

- Writing complete sentences rather than sentence fragments and run-on sentences that characterize spoken English
- Various aspects of the English verb system[3]
- The meaning and use of the English noun phrase
- The use of affixes (inflectional and derivational prefixes and suffixes)

Of course, the structures listed above (and all grammatical structures) should not be taught in isolation, nor should students use uncontextualized workbook exercises to practice them. Instead, these structures should rise from the context of the academic language that students are reading and writing about for each particular writing assignment. Moreover, the structures should be presented by teachers in different and increasingly difficult but authentic contexts as language proficiency and course level increase. In addition, grammar and vocabulary can be taught together: "When you write X, you use these words and these grammatical structures to communicate successfully."

"Power Grammar" and Academic Writing[4]

Each chapter in the Houghton Mifflin *English for Academic Success* writing student textbooks identifies and explains specific grammar structures used in the writing assignment(s) of that chapter.[5] Named "Power Grammar," the structures particular to the content and vocabulary of the discipline-specific chapters have been analyzed and presented so that students can practice those structures and use them in their writing.[6]

Teachers' Myths about Teaching Grammar to ESL EAP Students

Although teachers may not say some of the following aloud, these beliefs permeate surveys and personal interviews, teachers' informal conversations, and reviews of materials for these students. Therefore, it is best to set them out and then to discuss them.

Myths about Grammar and ESL EAP Student Writers

1. These students should enter their academic classes with accurate (even perfect) English.
2. Inaccurate English = lack of academic ability . . . and its corollary:
3. Language proficiency = student intelligence, knowledge.[7]
4. Students must learn ear-perfect grammar <u>before</u> they can learn to write.
5. Many students have been in the United States long enough to perfect their English.
6. If a student turns in a paper with accurate grammar, it may be someone else's work.
7. Students' language problems are mysterious and incomprehensible.

One logical consequence of these incorrect beliefs seems to be the decision to "improve" student grammar before teaching students to write, or at least to spend a substantial amount of class time teaching grammar in writing classes.

As counterintuitive as it may be, however, research indicates that teaching grammar by having NES or ESL students study English grammar rules and apply them to sentence-level exercises for remediation purposes is unsuccessful if the goal is to improve the grammar in their written work. That is, knowledge or understanding gained by doing fill-in-the-blank or sentence-level exercises does not seem to transfer successfully or efficiently into students' writing. Although the issue remains controversial, as early as

1963, authors of a "landmark research review" concluded that teaching such structured grammar rules to NES writers did not improve writing:

> In view of the wide-spread agreement of research studies based upon many types of students and teachers, the conclusion can be stated in strong and unqualified terms: the teaching of formal grammar has a negligible or, because it usually displaces some instruction and practice in composition, even a harmful effect on the improvement of writing.[8] (Braddock, Lloyd-Jones, & Shoer, pp. 37–38)

At the very least, the "cost-benefit" ratio is very low: a lot of teaching, a lot of worksheets, and very little visible improvement at best.

In fact, the problem of accuracy in L2 academic language may be even more difficult to remediate. For example, Merrill Swain and other Canadian researchers studied English-speaking children in Montreal (a bilingual city) who were "immersed" in French (L2) classes. After more than twenty years of research, ESL researchers Swain, Michael Long, and others reported that these French-immersion students, who were exposed to classroom learning in the L2 from their entrance into elementary school, developed native-like listening and high-quality reading skills.

However, "even at intermediate and higher grade levels they often [communicate] with non-target-like morphology and syntax."[9] In other words, these children were exposed to standard academic French daily for "more than 12 years of immersion at school and university in some cases" (Long & Robinson, 1998),[10] their oral communication skills became fluent (but not accurate), and their comprehension skills (e.g., reading and listening) became near-native-like. Their writing skills, however, "remain far from nativelike, particularly with respect to grammatical competence."[11] In the light of this groundbreaking research, we might reconsider the accuracy problems demonstrated in the writing of "ear" learners, who, like the Canadian students, were immersed in the world of English.

In addition to the belief that grammar exercises will improve the writing of L2 students, informal and formal surveys and personal interviews show that some (perhaps only a few) ESL EAP writing teachers harbor one or more of the following beliefs, each of which might work against students' successful remediation.[12]

Myths about Students in ESL EAP Writing Classes

1. Many of these students cannot learn quickly.
2. Their classroom behaviors often demonstrate lack of self-discipline.
3. The classroom attitudes of many indicate a lack of motivation.
4. Their English shows that they are remedial students.
5. They don't ask questions, so they must understand.
6. Many of these students plagiarize; therefore, they cheat, and they are untrustworthy.

Here, too, there seem to be logical curriculum consequences. Because these students have such "bad" English, and because they cannot seem to improve at a required rate, they should therefore be challenged to improve their grammar in order to improve their writing—or they should be allowed to fail.

Error, Grammar, and Resident Students

We know, however, that resident ESL writers have strengths—as speakers, as students, and as thinkers. Their oral competence is high, in language that is comprehensible by native English speakers, if not entirely accurate. They have wide and deep knowledge and understanding of idioms and what researchers call "lexical bundles" (word sets that commonly occur together such as *I don't know what . . ., one of the most, the nature of the . . .,* and *on the other hand . . .*).

They therefore may be the perfect student audience for teaching grammar, as Pat Byrd suggests, by (a) identifying the language of the "lexical bundles" and the particular contexts in which they are used and (b) "providing instructional materials that demonstrate and teach the language expected in those contexts."[13] We also know that labeling these students immature or unmotivated may be in error: instead, they may be afraid but acting "cool," as traditional-age, native-English speaking, U.S. high school graduates who have faced failures in writing might.

Better to learn more about the students and their grammar needs, discover the "set pieces" of academic language and teach that language to students, develop a process for informing them about and encouraging them to prioritize their errors, and teach them strategies to self-diagnose and self-prescribe solutions to their language problems.[14]

Grammar and U.S. EAP Resident Student Writers

One of the most important differences between the errors of international students and those of resident students is the types of errors made. Because of those differences, **the formal grammar taught to international students, which has been designed for "eye" learners who study English as a foreign language, is inappropriate and frustrating for U.S. resident student writers.** In addition, the scope and sequence of that grammar is inappropriate for L2 resident students for one or more of the following reasons (summarized from previous chapters):

- The errors of resident ear learners differ from those of eye learners both in types and in word categories. For example, resident ESL writers may already be writing complex structures correctly, but their spelling may be close to incomprehensible.
- The knowledge base of each group differs, and so the chronology of structures in ESL grammar textbooks is at best confusing, at worst irrelevant for many ear learners. Think, for example, of teaching fluent English speakers about the verb *to be* when (a) they have never noticed it before but they use it correctly and/or (b) they already fully understand this elementary lesson.
- Resident ear learners' errors may spring from different reasons and/or rules. This makes learning correct structures and rules more difficult.
- Similar to native English speakers and more similar to second dialect speakers (e.g., first language speakers of African American English dialect), ESL resident writers have very limited knowledge of grammatical terminology. If teachers assume such knowledge, resident ESL writers may "turn off" to grammar.
- If resident ear learners are semiliterate or illiterate in their L1s, they may have difficulty conceptualizing linguistically described structures.

Explanation

Pick up three or four ESL grammar textbooks and notice in the table of contents that the grammar structures are sequenced in similar order, especially at the lower levels of language proficiency. Steve Krashen's *Natural Order of Acquisition*,[15] which in some ways parallels the L1 acquisition of English, is often described as the "scientific" basis for this sequencing. As Pat Byrd and many others point out, however, there are many reasons to believe that the L2 acquisition of English probably differs, and differs dramatically, from L1 acquisition. These reasons include the previous background of the students (e.g., "ear" or "eye" learners) and the diverse languages and cultures of international or resident student learners.

What recent research has shown is that teaching grammar by "function" and "word category" is neither effective nor efficient. Yet current grammar books present structures by function: all verbs are taught together, all prepositions together, and so forth. Textbooks and teachers present inflectional groups or determiners or verb phrases, each separately, each without much consideration of frequency of use or range of use. Further, the word *this* receives the same amount of time as the word *that*, although the latter is used four times as often in spoken English. Students may learn relationships among verbs or inflectional suffixes but not the bonds between, for instance, other grammar and vocabulary features of English.[16]

Teaching Grammar "Patterns"

Discourse research describes how English is used in context—in real life. Discourse analysis (computer text-analysis of continuous stretches of language beyond the sentence level—i.e., language "in context") by Doug Biber and others has demonstrated another way to organize the presentation of grammar structures. Here are some of the "patterns" Biber's research has identified:

1. Patterns of usage
   a. In academic writing, use of complex noun phrases
   b. In spoken English, use of personal pronouns
2. Words that are used together frequently (called "collocation")
   a. Phrases such as "salt and pepper"
   b. Idioms such as "wreaking havoc," "made good time"
   c. Verb particles such as "lighten up," "get away with"
3. Grammatical patterns in written genres and other unifying patterns
   a. History writing: appositives, definitions, proper nouns, pronouns
   b. Accounting writing: present tense verbs, generic noun phrases[17]

The discovery of grammatical patterns and word collocations puts the teaching focus of grammatical structures on meaning and communication needed by the students. For example, as Pat Byrd points out, when students write reports for academic classes, they need to learn the language used to report other people's information. That includes:

1. Summary writing (see Chapter 12 for additional discussion):
   a. Verbs such as *find, mention, say, report,* and so on
   b. Noun clauses (often used as objects to the verbs above)
   c. Complex (but not compound) sentences
2. Quotations: adverbials to introduce and connect the ideas of others

This approach fulfills vocabulary specialist Paul Nation's definition: knowledge of a word includes knowledge of the grammar (i.e., the patterns and the collocations) associated with the use of that word.[18]

Given the information about grammar patterns, we can form two assumptions about preparing to teach grammar in the writing course:

1. Students need to learn about grammar structures that they must use in U.S. academic writing, structures that they may have encountered in their academic reading but have not produced successfully.[19]
2. Relearning or remediating error is more difficult and more time-consuming than learning new material, but students can learn to identify, to monitor their writing for, and even to correct their habituated language errors.

How to Select Grammar Structures to Teach[20]

Because resident ESL writers have been more or less immersed in the English language, they have been exposed to a great variety of grammar structures. Consequently, instead of dividing grammar into "levels" of L1 acquisition patterns or even of perceived level of difficulty or frequency, we need to look at current research that analyzes discourse: Simply put, the grammar taught in writing classes should be structures that:

1. Students will encounter in their academic textbooks and writing assignments
2. Students will use in their academic writing

It follows that grammar structures, even at lower levels of language proficiency, should be selected <u>from</u> grammar patterns (clusters) in the reading and writing that students are required to do. Pat Byrd's research shows:

1. Grammar examples should be authentic (not constructed by the teacher, not "adapted" from another source), even at the lower levels of language proficiency so that students learn to read and write language they will encounter in their academic experiences. Teacher-constructed or "adapted" prose defeats the purpose of teaching grammar.
2. Grammar structures from authentic academic writing that mirrors the type of writing the student is assigned in the chapter (e.g., comparing historical events, explaining the causes of a disease, arguing for a solution to an environmental problem) should be the focus for teaching. [21]

Explanation

For example, if students are learning about writing academic reports, and the theme of the chapter is "college stress," the reading(s) and the student samples in the chapter will almost certainly include the use of a "cluster" of such grammar structures as:

1. Sentences that report information
2. Report verbs

and perhaps

3. Direct quotations
4. Appositives (to identify sources)[22]

Notice that structures not listed are oral English structures, including the syntax of questions, the use of contractions, informal or idiomatic language and structures, the use of personal pronouns, and "ritual language" such as greetings, apologies, and the like. These structures, though relevant to spoken English, are irrelevant for academic writing (and besides, ear learners may already be proficient in these oral structures).

Using Discourse Analysis Results to Select and Prioritize

Discourse analysts like Doug Biber have demonstrated empirically that, in speaking and in writing, particular features of grammar are "clustered" together. For example, in what Biber calls "informational communication" (as opposed to "involved" or personal communication) the following grammar structures occur frequently:

1. Verbs
   a. Very few verbs (i.e., not many "different" verbs)
   b. The same verbs repeated often
   c. A high use of the verbs *to be* and *to have*
   d. The frequent use of agentless passives
2. Nouns and noun phrases
   a. Many different nouns
   b. Often, noun phrases are longer than nouns and noun phrases used in more personal communication
   c. "Attributive" adjectives (those adjectives that come in front of a noun)
   d. Heavy use of multiple prepositional phrases to modify nouns
   e. Present and past participial phrases (often to add additional information to nouns)
   f. "Place" adverbials used to indicate location (*here, there*)[23]

Notice from the previous list two important grammar concepts for academic student writers:

1. Although students need not know extensive "verb vocabulary," learning "noun vocabulary" seems essential.
2. Informational writing contains long, complex noun phrases, so students should learn as much about them as possible, beginning with simpler noun phrases at lower levels of language proficiency.

Explanation

Following are additional examples of academic grammar "from context" that linguist Pat Byrd has drawn from Doug Biber's discourse analyses. For example, Biber's discourse analysis results show grammar clusters in a more specialized form of informational language: the language of definitions. The examples Byrd gives are from a widely used intermediate accounting textbook.

1. Present tense verbs: "Liabilities **are** . . .," "Gains **are** increases . . ."
2. Generic noun phrases used to name concepts or terms: "**Teachers** are underpaid," "**Lead** is not used in pencils," "**Distributions to owners** are decreases in . . ."
3. Sentence structure: **Term** + verb **TO BE** + **complex noun phrase** (verb complement)
4. Numerous prepositional phrases attached to nouns: "Losses are decreases **in equity** (net assets) **from peripheral** or incidental **transactions of an entity** . . ."
5. Use of logical (instead of chronological) connections (transitions): "Expenses are outflows **or** other using-up of assets **or** incurrences . . ."

Strategies for Prioritizing Remediation of Language Errors

Although teachers can be responsible for introducing new grammatical structures that will be useful for the academic writing their students do. However, students still face the sticky, time-consuming, and frustrating task of remediation of language error. In this case, teachers can act as experts and coaches: identifying and prioritizing error types and encouraging and supporting students in their attempts to remediate. Much of the remediation of error is individual, not classroom, work, but teachers can provide information about error gravity, remediation strategies, and campus resources that will help students remediate their individual errors.

As discussed in Chapters 5 and 21, some errors are important and "treatable," whereas others are less important and nearly impossible to remediate in a semester (or a year). Students are usually relieved to learn about "error gravity": they can narrow their remediation to "grievous" errors and develop specific strategies that will enable them to select and prioritize their study.

For example, once errors have been identified, teachers might suggest that students concentrate on two major errors for the semester, and then discuss strategies for correcting these errors. Students may find it helpful to list or catalog their individual errors. By using an error chart (see Chapter 17 for an example), they can see that they make systematic and perhaps even rule-governed errors. One successful example of using a single focused structure is explained in a recent article.[24] The researchers worked with ESL students in two middle school science classes where they focused explicitly on past tense verbs that are used in laboratory reports.

As teacher-trainer John Bean states, "To change, we do not need grammar lessons so much as behavior modification, perhaps by enlisting . . . a friend to stop us . . . [from] social embarrassment."[25] Or by taping a list of frequently used and misspelled words in the bathroom or over a sink that the student uses regularly. Or by planning a prioritized study of regular verb endings and practicing with a peer.

Another student-based strategy for identifying and correcting errors needs a "listener." That is, reading their writing aloud seems to help U.S. resident students "hear" errors; research indicates they often (unconsciously) correct some of their errors as they read. But for readers who do not hear their corrections, a teacher in conference with the student, or a native English-speaking peer, can identify those changes for the student writer as he or she reads a piece of writing aloud.

Conclusion

Despite the caveats of this chapter, grammar structures can be taught in the composition classroom, and students can remediate habitual errors in their writing. Of course, we need to put students' language needs first with authentic language and pedagogic tasks that help us make rational, principled decisions about the focus of grammar instruction. Further, it is essential that students **notice** particular grammar structures in order to learn about and practice them.

To summarize:

1. Workbook grammar exercises almost certainly do not improve students' academic writing.
2. Written errors by U.S. resident students should be seen by their instructors in the context of interlanguage and communicative purpose.

3. Student writing errors need to be prioritized if the writers are to benefit from remediation strategies, and students should be aware of the concept of "error gravity."

4. Some errors are almost never 100 percent remediable. Fortunately, these errors do not usually interfere with reader comprehension; unfortunately, they are immediately visible and irritating to academic readers.

5. For such errors (in particular, articles and prepositions, and perhaps some inflections), U.S. resident writers should spend their time more wisely on content and organization of their ideas and on other, more serious errors. Then they should ask a native speaker of English for assistance in identifying and correcting the articles and prepositions (and perhaps inflections) in their writing.

Endnotes

1. Ferris, D. (1999). The case for grammar correction in L2 writing classes: A response to Truscott (1996). *Journal of Second Language Writing, 8,* 1–10.
2. Hinkel, E. (2002). *Second language writers' text: Linguistic and rhetorical features.* Mahwah, NJ: Erlbaum.
3. Bardovi-Harlig, K. (2000). *Tense and aspect in second language acquisition: Form, meaning, and use.* Malden, MA: Blackwell.
4. For an introduction to Power Grammar, see the end of Chapter 12.
5. In other words, each Power Grammar section reflects the research of Diane Larsen-Freeman, that "forms" get their "meanings" when used in particular contexts.
6. For more specific information about integrating grammar structures with student writing, see Dana Ferris' groundbreaking book, *Treatment of Error in Second Language Writing* (2002). Ann Arbor: University of Michigan Press.
7. Vollmer, G. (2000). Praise and stigma: Teachers' construction of the typical ESL student. *Journal of Intercultural Studies, 21,* 53–66.
8. Braddock, R., Lloyd-Jones, R., & Shoer, L. (1963). *Research in written composition* (pp. 37–38). Champagne, IL: National Council of Teachers of English.
9. Swain, M. (1998). Focus on form through conscious reflection. In C. Doughty & J. Williams (Eds.), *Focus on form in classroom second language acquisition* (pp. 64–81). Cambridge, UK: Cambridge University Press. (p. 65.)
10. Long, M., & Robinson, P. (1998). Focus on form: Theory, research, and practice. In C. Doughty & J. Williams (Eds.), *Focus on form in classroom second language acquisition* (pp. 15–41). Cambridge, UK: Cambridge University Press. (pp. 20–21.)

11. Swain, M. (1991). French immersion and its offshoots: Getting two for one. In B. Freed (Ed.), *French language acquisition: Research and the classroom* (pp. 91–103). Lexington, MA: Heath.

12. My reviewer indicates that she has not heard any but the last of these myths. I include them because research shows that they exist.

13. Byrd, P. (2005a). Instructed grammar. In E. Hinkel (Ed.), *Handbook of second language teaching and learning.* Mahwah, NJ: Erlbaum.

14. Hinkel, E., & Fotos, S. (Eds.). (2001). *New perspectives on grammar teaching in the second language classroom.* Mahwah, NJ: Erlbaum.

15. Krashen, S., & Terrell, T. (1982). *The natural order of acquisition.* San Francisco: Alemany Press.

16. Byrd, P. (1994). Writing grammar textbooks: Theory and practice. *System, 22*(2), 245–255.

17. Biber, D., Conrad, S., Reppen, R., Byrd, P., & Helt, M. (2002). Speaking and writing in the university: A multidimensional comparison. *TESOL Quarterly, 36*(1), 9–48.

18. Nation, I. S. P. (1990). *Teaching and learning vocabulary.* Boston: Heinle & Heinle.

19. Byrd, P. (1988). Rethinking grammar at various proficiency levels: Implications of authentic materials for the EAP curriculum. In J. Reid & P. Byrd (Eds.), *Grammar in the composition classroom* (pp. 69–97). Boston: Heinle & Heinle.

20. Byrd (2005a).

21. Byrd, P. (2005b). Nouns without articles: Focusing instruction for ESL/EFL learners with the context of authentic discourse. In J. Frodesen & C. Holton (Eds.), *The power of context in language teaching and learning.* Boston: Heinle & Heinle.

22. To read and analyze a student essay about the topic of college stress, see the Houghton Mifflin website www.college.hmco.com/esl/instructors.

23. Biber, D. (1988). *Variation across speech and writing.* New York: Cambridge University Press.

24. Doughty, C., & Williams, J. (1998). *Focus on form in classroom second language acquisition.* Cambridge, UK: Cambridge University Press.

25. Bean, J. C. (2001). *Engaging ideas: The professor's guide to integrating writing, critical thinking, and active learning in the classroom.* San Francisco: Jossey-Bass.

Index